SUPER PSYCHOLOGY

METRO BOOKS
New York

An Imprint of Sterling Publishing Co., Inc.
1166 Avenue of the Americas
New York, NY 10036

ISBN 978-1-4351-6462-8

For information about custom editions, special sales, and premium and corporate purchases,
please contact Sterling Special Sales at 800-805-5489 or specialsales@sterlingpublishing.com.

Manufactured in China

2 4 6 8 10 9 7 5 3 1

www.sterlingpublishing.com

Credits: Interior layouts by Alyssa Peacock

SUPER
PSYCHOLOGY

A TOTALLY NON-SCARY GUIDE TO PSYCHOLOGY AND WHAT IT MEANS

Christian Jarrett & Joannah Ginsburg

METRO BOOKS

NEW YORK

Contents

"The truly horrifying idea is that what we think we know, what we believe with all our hearts, is not necessarily the truth.**"**

—Loftus speaking to *Psychology Today* magazine, 1996

What Is Psychology?

Psychology isn't mind reading. It doesn't only focus on people with mental-health problems. And it isn't just about body language. Psychology is a diverse science of the mind and of behavior, as well as a thriving profession.

Since the dawn of ancient civilizations in China, India, Egypt, and Greece, great thinkers have been asking questions about the human mind and why people behave as they do. But it's only relatively recently that scholars have taken a scientific approach to these issues, leading to the birth of psychology (literally the "study of the mind," from the Greek *psyche*, meaning mind, and *logos*, meaning study).

A scientific approach means forming predictions, observing, and testing those predictions, before repeating the whole exercise to check the results. Anyone can make a claim about human behavior: "If you smile, it makes you feel happier," but only psychologists will test that claim with precise experiments. They'll recruit participants and think of sensitive ways to measure mood. They'll consider possible alternative influences—for instance, perhaps any kind of exercise of the facial muscles improves mood? The psychologists will make sure they test not only the effects of smiling but also the impact of frowning or chewing.

Probably the earliest person to investigate mental processes scientifically was Wilhelm Wundt, founder of the world's first psychology lab in Leipzig, Germany, in 1879. Wundt's theory of Structuralism sought to break down consciousness into its component parts. Although his approach brought more precision to the study of the mind, he still used introspection, which, because of its subjective nature, is not seen as very scientific.

····Wilhelm Wundt

The twentieth century brought with it a new rigorously scientific field of psychology—behaviorism. Its founder, U.S. psychologist John Watson, believed psychology could only claim to be a science if it focused strictly on outwardly observable behavior.

Behaviorism's influence meant that it was the middle of the twentieth century before experimental psychologists, inspired by developments in computer science, began to focus once again on mental processes.

Areas of Psychology

Social psychology seeks to understand how we interact with each other and looks at issues such as prejudice and embarrassment. Developmental psychology studies the learning and maturation of infants and children. Cognitive psychology focuses on information processing: how we perceive the world and talk about it. Cognitive neuropsychology looks at how brain damage affects these mental faculties. Comparative psychology studies non-human animal behavior. There's biological psychology, which investigates how our physical bodies affect how we behave, looking at functions such as sleeping and stress. Occupational psychology studies behavior at work, while health psychology looks at our response to illness. Of course many psychologists also study mental illness, including anxiety, depression, and psychosis.

More recent areas of psychology include environmental psychology, which tackles the ways in which the environment affects our behavior and how we affect it. There's parapsychology, which studies unusual experiences, and criminological psychology, which examines criminal behavior and police techniques. One of the newest areas is positive psychology, which aims to understand human growth and achievement.

Modern Psychological Techniques

Many psychological techniques have changed little over the years. You still can't beat asking someone how they feel or what they believe about something. But probably the biggest change over the last few decades has come from the development of brain-imaging techniques such as magnetic resonance imaging (MRI) and positron emission tomography (PET). These still don't directly measure human thought, but they do provide a window on the biological workings of the mind. Another relatively new technique is transcranial magnetic stimulation (TMS), which allows psychologists to temporarily knock out a specific region of a healthy person's brain.

A **magnetic resonance imaging** (MRI) scan of a brain.

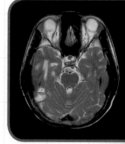

Developmental psychology focuses on **children**.

Types of Psychologists

As the science of psychology beavers away, uncovering what makes us tick, many psychologists take what we've learned so far out into the world for the betterment of society. Clinical and counseling psychologists use evidence-based therapeutic techniques to help people with mental problems. Business psychologists help companies improve productivity and staff morale. Forensic psychologists help rehabilitate offenders and advise the police. Educational psychologists help children at school, especially those with learning difficulties. Sports psychologists work with teams and athletes to help them reach their peak performance. Meanwhile, health psychologists help people cope with illness and advise on health care and promotion.

Buckle up and get comfy—you're about to be taken on a roller-coaster ride through popular psychology:

1. Perception and Action takes a look at how we're plugged into the world via our senses and includes some neat illusions that show how our brains sometimes make mistakes.

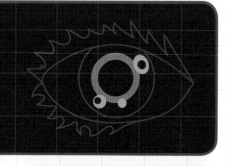

2. Memory takes a journey through our mental archives, including some tips on boosting your memory abilities and a survey of recent research on whether bad memories can be erased.

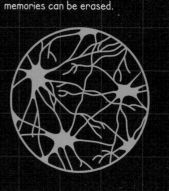

3. Cognition gets inside your mind, showing you're not as rational as you thought and looking at problems some people have with language and counting.

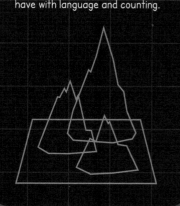

4. Affect may challenge some of your basic ideas on human behavior and communication patterns, exploring animal instincts and personality traits.

6. Personality puts the spotlight on you, with a range of tests that should help you get to know yourself better.

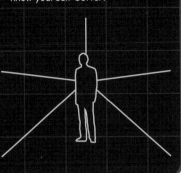

5. The Social Self recognizes that we're social beings, rounds up research on relationships, as well as putting leadership and brainstorming under the microscope.

7. Stress and Anxiety shows the strange ways our brains and bodies can react when we are faced with especially intense or traumatic situations.

8. Sleep explores the fascinating and complicated relationship of mind and body, helping us understand what we may learn about ourselves through our dreams, explaining phenomena such as sleepwalking, and providing tips on how to be more in touch with your dreaming self and how to get better sleep!

Zzz

Throughout the chapters you'll find mini features on some key psychologists who have worked in these fields.

1

Perception and Action

Our sensory pathways communicate a whirlwind of data about the world to the brain, which is essentially a meaty information-processing machine. This chapter, covering vision, hearing, touch, and more, is about how the brain makes sense of all that information and uses it to decide how to act. But everything is not always as it seems, as we'll discover with illusions and other phenomena.

Seeing

As you glance about, enjoying all the richness of the visual world, it is easy to underestimate the complex journey that makes sight possible. It starts with light rays hitting a screen of photo-receptive cells at the back of your eyes— the retina—where the light is turned into a neural signal. Next comes the optic nerve, which carries the visual information on to a relay station, the lateral geniculate nucleus, from where it is wired to the sprawling visual cortex at the back of your brain. Curiously, the left-hand side of your brain processes the right side of space, and the right-hand side of your brain processes the left half.

The Science of Sight

Beyond the first stage of the visual cortex, known as primary visual cortex or V1, the processing of visual information is split into two parts, for the purposes of either performing actions or perceiving what things are. This has been demonstrated through the observation of patients

THE VISUAL PROJECTION PATHWAY

A cross-section through the **brain** illustrating the visual system, which is made up of the optic nerve, the optic chiasm, and the visual cortex.

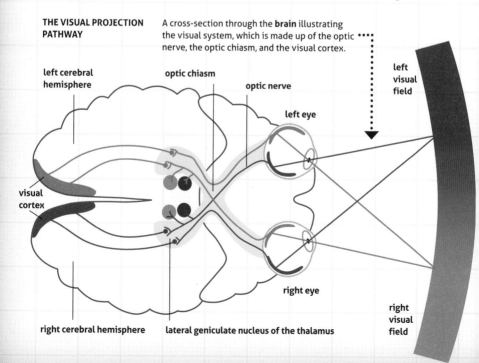

left cerebral hemisphere

optic chiasm

optic nerve

left eye

left visual field

visual cortex

right eye

right cerebral hemisphere

lateral geniculate nucleus of the thalamus

right visual field

with damage to one pathway or the other. For example, the psychologists David Milner and Melvyn Goodale described the case of patient D. F., who, with her damaged "perception" stream, was unable to say which way a post-box type slot was orientated, yet was perfectly capable of "posting" letters into the slot by angling her delivery correctly.

Light-sensitive cells on your retina are not distributed evenly but are concentrated in the center, in a region called the fovea. This is one of the reasons you need to move your eyes around, so that you can focus objects of interest on this area. There are also two types of retinal cells—rods for seeing shades of gray in dim light, and cones for processing color. Rods tend to be concentrated more in the outer region of your retina, which is why, in the dark, you might actually find it easier to see something by looking just to one side of it rather than straight on.

Eye Movements

The eye movement you make most often is called a saccade. These are the jerky, jumpy movements people make when they are reading. A little-known fact is that when you move your eyes in this way, your vision is actually shut down temporarily, to stop the visual scene blurring with the thousands of these movements you make every day. Because saccadic eye movements are so fast, typically lasting less than

---

TRY OUT THE "STOPPED CLOCK EFFECT"

Find a clock—an old-fashioned one with hands is better, as long as it doesn't tick, but a digital one will also do so long as it shows seconds. Now place the clock to one side and glance over at the second hand (or digits). The clock must be far enough away so that you have to shift your eyes to see it. You might need to try this a few times, but you should eventually notice that the second hand seems to hang still for too long, as though the clock has stopped momentarily.

One explanation for why this happens is that, in order to compensate for the visual suppression that occurs during eye movements, your brain effectively backdates how long it believes an object has been in its current position. This works fine when you glance at an inanimate object like a desk or book, but it can cause a strange sensation when you glance at an object such as a second hand which you know doesn't stay still for too long.

---

a quarter of a second, you don't usually notice this effect, but there is an illusion, called the "Stopped Clock Effect," which some experts have suggested is caused by this brief visual shut-down.

Watching Things Move

Being able to see when things are moving is vital to our survival. We wouldn't have lasted long on the open savanna if we hadn't been able to notice that lion bounding toward us, or our potential dinner running off.

What Is Motion?

Motion is literally a change in position over time, and you detect movement when the image of an object or animal moves across the cells of your retina. However, there are all sorts of complicated calculations involved in motion perception because to tell whether other things are moving you have to factor in your own movements—those of your body through space, and also of your eyes.

Usually when you move your eyes, the motor command for the eye movement is copied and used to cancel out any resulting movement of images across the retina. However, if you move one of your eyes using a gentle nudge of your finger against your eyeball, you'll see that in this case the world does appear to move. This is because you moved your eye externally with your finger, so there wasn't an internal "eye movement command" to cancel out.

Motion Blindness

In 1983, neuropsychology professor Josef Zihl described the case of a 43-year-old woman who lost the ability to see motion (known as akinetopsia) after suffering strokes on both sides of her brain. She retained her ability to recognize objects and words, and could even detect the movement of sounds through space, or the movement of an object up and down her arm. However, she couldn't pour drinks because the fluid appeared frozen in mid-air, and crossing the road was particularly hazardous. Her strokes caused damage to a region of her brain—referred to by psychologists as visual area V5—that is selectively activated when we look at motion.

The Waterfall Illusion

There are plenty of fun illusions that each reveal something different about the way we process motion.

Probably the most famous is the "waterfall illusion." If you haven't got a waterfall handy, you need to find something large that is constantly moving in one direction, such as a luggage carousel or a river flowing by.

Stare at the waterfall for a good 30 seconds or so and then look away. You'll see that the rocks to the side of the fall appear to rush upward in the opposite direction to the waterfall. It's thought that cells sensitive to the downward direction of the waterfall become desensitized and cause this effect. Normally, cells sensitive to different directions are in a kind of balanced opposition, but once the waterfall fatigues the downwardly sensitive cells, the upwardly sensitive cells dominate and lead us to see upward motion that isn't really there.

The Flash Lag Effect

One problem when it comes to viewing moving objects is the fact

that it takes a certain amount of time for neural signals carrying visual information to travel through the brain. So by the time we've finished processing a moving object in its current position, it will actually be somewhere else further along its trajectory. This effect is demonstrated in a phenomenon known as the "Flash Lag Effect" in which a briefly flashed stationary object appears to lag behind its moving partner, even though both objects are really in alignment.

One explanation for this effect is that in order to compensate for neural processing delays, our brains actually locate moving objects slightly ahead of their true position. This process isn't applied to stationary objects, hence the way the stationary, flashed object appears to lag behind the moving one.

Blindspots and Blindsight

We tend to think that a blind person must have something wrong with their eyes, but people with healthy eyes who suffer damage to the primary visual cortex can also experience what's known as "cortical blindness." In this case, part of their visual cortex will often remain intact so that they can see one half of the visual world but not the other. A curious phenomenon called "blindsight" occurs in these patients, in which they are able to determine the characteristics of objects placed in their blind visual field, even though they report not being able to see anything there.

A series of experiments by British psychologist Lawrence Weiskrantz has shown that patients with blindsight can determine object color, location, shape, and brightness, and even the emotional expression of faces, in their blind field.

In one test, if a patient is asked to respond as fast as possible to the sight of a square in their healthy field, the presentation of an identical square in their blind field should, if processed, speed their performance. And that's exactly what's been found, further suggesting that some residual visual processing still occurs in the blind half of the patient's vision.

It's most likely that this residual visual ability relies on parts of the visual pathway that bypass the damaged primary visual cortex, and feed instead straight into subcortical visual areas, such as the superior colliculus—areas whose processing isn't accessible to consciousness. Another possibility is that these patients have islands of intact primary visual cortex underlying their residual abilities.

Visual Neglect

Another neuropsychological condition that is reminiscent of blindsight is known as visual neglect. In this case there is nothing wrong with the patients' eyes or the visual parts of their brain, but damage to

Blindsight patients respond faster to a shape flashed in their healthy field of vision when an identical shape is also presented to their blind field.

the parietal cortex (usually on the right-hand side), near the crown of the head, leads them to completely ignore half of the world, on the side opposite their injury, as if it doesn't exist.

The condition can manifest itself in striking ways. For example, patients will shave just one side of their face, eat from just one side of their dinner plate, or draw a clock with all the numbers on one side missing. However, in a similar way to blindsight, there is evidence that such patients do process some aspects of the part of space that they ignore. Asked whether an object presented in their affected field is the same as an object presented to their intact field, they will perform better than you'd expect if they were just guessing.

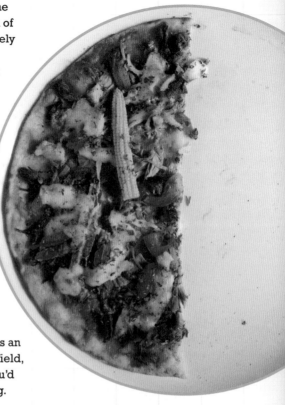

FIND YOUR OWN BLINDSPOT

In a sense, you are blind to a part of your visual world too, thanks to what is known as the blindspot or scotoma in each of your eyes. You have a blindspot because there is a gap in your retina, through which the fibers of your photo-receptive cells leave your eye to form the optic nerve. Any light falling on this area is not processed.

We're not normally aware of our two blindspots because our brains "fill in" the missing information. However, you can find out where your blindspot is by closing your left eye and looking at the cross below. Stay focused on the cross, and as you move the book gradually closer to you, or further away, at some point the circle on the right will disappear.

Touch

....

Touch begins in our skin, which is packed with receptors that each respond to pressure, temperature, or pain. These skin receptors feed into the spinal cord, which snakes the messages up toward the brain from where our actual sensation of touch arises. We have other sensors in our muscles too—these are for what is called proprioception, which is the sense of where the parts of our body are located in space.

A still little-understood aspect of touch is itch. This sensation depends on the same nerve pathways that carry pain sensations, and to many people an unreachable itch can be a real pain. In fact there are reports of patients who experience itchiness so excruciating that they prefer the pain of scratching themselves until they bleed to the discomfort of an itch.

Scratching at a nagging itch can be immensely satisfying.

THE HOMUNCULUS (LATIN FOR "LITTLE MAN")

Inside your brain, there's a voodoo-doll-like representation of your body, which is activated when the corresponding part of your real body is touched. It's like a little you in your brain, except that each body part isn't to scale. Instead, the amount of neural tissue given over to each limb, finger, or nose depends on the sensitivity of the skin on that part of your body. The "little you" inside your head isn't arranged quite as you are in real life either— for example, the cells that represent your feet are found near those cells that respond when your genitals are touched!

Exaggerated **hands** and **lips** reflect the most sensitive areas of the body.

The Social Side of Touch

Increasingly, research is uncovering just how important touch can be to our psychological well-being. For example, baby orphans deprived of human contact are more likely to die than those who are held. Touch can also be persuasive. In a paper published in 2007 in the journal *Social Influence*, French psychologist Nicolas Guéguen described how three male research assistants approached 240 women in the street and asked them for their phone numbers. Among those 120 women whom the researchers touched lightly on the arm, 19 percent agreed to share their number, compared with just 10 percent of the women with whom no physical contact was made. Furthermore, when a researcher approached women in a nightclub, of those he touched lightly on the arm, 65 percent agreed to a dance, compared with just 43 percent of those he asked without making any physical contact.

Most people respond • • • • • •
positively to gentle
touch, even
from a
stranger.

The Rubber Hand Illusion

Our sense of touch is strongly affected by our sense of sight. We seem to know this instinctively— think of how many people look away when they're having a vaccine jab. The way sight and touch work together can be shown with the help of a rubber hand (or a stuffed rubber glove), a table, and two feathers. Place one hand on top of the table and your other hand underneath the table so you can't see it. Then place the rubber hand on the table, parallel with your real hand. Ask a friend to stroke the hand under the table and the rubber hand with the two feathers, with the exact same rhythm and timing. If you keep watching the rubber hand being stroked, while your real hand is stroked under the table, you should eventually experience the alarming sensation that the rubber hand is part of you! The illusion shows how vision can override your proprioceptive sense of where your hand is, remapping the feeling of being stroked to the location of the rubber hand.

Hearing

....

It's presumably very quiet on the airless moon because sound is the vibration of air, or some other medium, which causes the eardrum at the end of your auditory canal to vibrate. This, in turn, causes the three bones of your middle ear to move to the same beat—these are the smallest bones in your body—and they transmit the noise to your inner ear, to the cochlea, where the auditory nerves are found.

When it comes to hearing you have just the two ears planted firmly on either side of your face. So to identify where sounds are coming from, your brain uses two tricks: One is to compare the loudness of a single sound as it arrives at each ear. The second is to compare the time the sound arrives. A sound from straight ahead will arrive at each ear at the same time, but a sound from the left will obviously arrive at your left ear sooner than the right and vice versa.

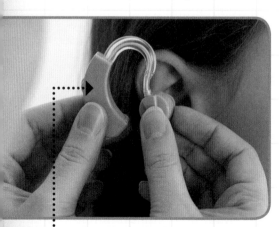

Complete deafness is extremely rare, and in general there are two types of hearing loss. Blockage to the auditory canal, or problems with the little bones of the middle ear, is known as conductive deafness and is usually easy to rectify with surgery or hearing aids. Trouble with the inner ear, however, is more difficult to remedy and is known as nerve deafness or inner-ear deafness.

A **hearing aid** helps to amplify sounds for those suffering from hearing loss.

Sight and Sound

On the flip side, there is increasing evidence that blind people have enhanced hearing, probably thanks to the auditory part of their brain hijacking the redundant neural tissue normally given over to seeing.

In 2007, a surprising study by Jörg Lewald suggested this hearing enhancement can also occur when sighted people are deprived of vision for short periods. He tested the ability of 20 blindfolded participants to say which stereo speaker had emitted a noise. As expected, they tended to say the sounds were more central than they really were. But then the participants sat blindfolded for 90 minutes before being tested again. This time, their performance was more accurate, and similar to the performance of blind participants. Crucially, this advantage wasn't just caused by practice at the task—participants who wore a blindfold only during testing didn't show the same improvement.

Depriving sighted people of vision can sharpen their hearing skills.

THE McGURK EFFECT

We saw in the section on touch (pp. 18–19) how vision can override your proprioceptive sense of where your hand is located. The McGurk Effect, first described by cognitive psychologist Harry McGurk, shows how visual information can be blended with auditory information, so that what you experience reflects a sensory combination quite different from what any one sense would have told you on its own. In this illusion, the sound of a person saying one thing (for example, the sound "BA") is played over a video showing their lips saying something else (for example, "GA"), with the result that you hear them saying a mixture of the two (for example, "DA").

The McGurk Effect tricks your brain's multisensory strategy that in other circumstances—such as trying to listen to your friend at a noisy party—helps you interpret what they're saying.

A similar phenomenon is described by neurologist Oliver Sacks in his book *Seeing Voices*. When the post-lingually deaf (those who have lost their hearing after having experienced the sound of spoken language) read people's lips, they sometimes experience the sound of the words that person is speaking. Sacks suggests that they are not just imagining what the sounds are like, but rather that the sight of the lip movements is automatically translated by their brains into the corresponding "phantasmal voices."

Moving

Deliberate intentions to move are formed in the brain's motor cortex, a spongy strip of gray matter that runs parallel to the neural body map that's responsible for your sense of touch. The motor cortex speaks to the spinal cord and from here the message is routed via elongated neurons to the appropriate muscles of the body.

It sounds straightforward enough, but a key problem with moving successfully is overcoming the sluggishness of your nerve signals. It takes time for sensory information to find its way into the brain, and added to that is the time it takes motor commands to reach your muscles. This means quite often you're not actually moving in response to the world as you see it, but rather in response to how you think it's going to be.

The Broken Escalator Phenomenon

A great example of your brain anticipating what movements it thinks it needs to make occurs when you're confronted by a broken escalator. Although you know the escalator is broken, your brain's autopilot still kicks in to compensate for the unnatural forward movement that it's expecting. But because the escalator isn't moving, the automatic commands sent to your legs and body to help keep your balance actually end up making you wobble a little, which can feel really strange.

When you step on to an escalator, your brain signals your body to prepare for the anticipated movement.

You Can't Tickle Yourself

As well as anticipating movements that you'll need to make, another trick your brain performs is to predict the outcome of your own actions. It does this to help overcome delays in sensory feedback and also to distinguish your own actions from those of other people or animals.

A clear demonstration of this comes from the fact that you can't tickle yourself. Go on, give it a try! Psychologist Sarah-Jayne Blakemore has performed a number of experiments on this topic. One had participants attempt to tickle their right hand using a robotic interface with soft foam on the end controlled by their left hand. When the interface and their left hand moved at the same time, the sensation didn't feel at all tickly. But then the researchers introduced a delay between the movement of the left hand and the tickling action of the foam, and they found the greater the delay, the more it tickled—it felt more like it was being performed by someone else.

This research suggests that when you move, a copy of the motor command is created so that its consequences can be labeled as self-generated. In other words, tickling doesn't work because the resulting sensation is anticipated and canceled out. But it seems that all it takes to disrupt this process is a little time delay.

Who's in Charge Anyway?

We've already seen that your brain can take over when faced with an unusual obstacle like an escalator. But presumably "you" are in control the majority of the time, right? Well, actually, maybe not. A classic study conducted by neuroscientist Benjamin Libet suggests that our sense of deciding when to move actually comes after the neural preparation for that movement has begun. Participants watched a second hand on a clock and made a mental note of the moment they decided to move their finger, which they duly moved. At the same time, Libet was measuring their brain activity by recording electrical changes via electrodes placed on the scalp. Libet's amazing discovery was that the spike in electrical activity normally associated with preparing to make a movement actually came a good 300–500 milliseconds prior to when the participants said they had decided to move.

A Sensory Cocktail

Can you imagine if words always had a certain taste? Or if numbers and letters were always tinged with color? That's exactly what life is like for people with synesthesia, who seem to experience a crossover of their senses resulting in a cocktail of sensations.

The most common type of synesthete is the "letter colorer," but there are many variations. Psychologist Jamie Ward described the case of one synesthete, J. I. W., who had to give some of his friends nicknames because their real names conjured up unpleasant tastes. Other synesthetes experience smells when musical notes are played.

Synesthesia was first described by Francis Galton, a pioneer in eugenics, in the late nineteenth century. He noticed that the condition appears to run in families, suggesting that it has a genetic basis.

In rare cases, synesthesia can be acquired through illness or can be induced by taking drugs such as LSD.

Some experts have doubted whether synesthetes really do have the sensory experiences they claim. But a large body of evidence has now built up, which overwhelmingly suggests synesthesia is real. For example, synesthetes have been tested on a version of the Stroop test, which requires participants to say what ink color a letter is written in. Consider a synesthete who says the letter "A" evokes the color red. If the synesthesia is real, then this person should be quicker to identify when the letter "A" is written in red ink than when it is written in blue ink, because the former situation is congruent with their synesthetic experience. And that's exactly what the studies have shown.

Psychologist Julia Nunn and her colleagues have also scanned the brains of synesthetes for whom words were tinged with color. The researchers found that activity was indeed sparked in the part of the brain that processes color when these participants were presented with words, but not when they were played auditory tones, thus supporting their subjective claims. By contrast, when a control group of participants were tested on the same task, the color-processing part of their brain wasn't activated by the words or tones.

For some **synesthetes** a particular musical note may conjure up a strong smell or taste.

A Mixing of Senses or Concepts?

. . . .

More recently, psychologists have been putting effort into explaining the synesthetic experience. This research is showing that synesthesia might not be a purely sensory experience but could have more to do with concepts.

For example, when Julia Simner and colleagues at Edinburgh University randomly tested around 1,700 people, they found not only that the condition was far more common than previously expected, with one in twenty claiming synesthetic status, but that concept-based versions

were the most common. For instance, some people reported that the days of the week or the months of the year were associated with certain colors.

With findings like these, psychologists have realized synesthesia could shed light on language processes common to all of us. For example, the experiences of synesthete J. I. W., mentioned above, have helped answer the question of whether letters of the alphabet are processed differently by the brain depending on how they are pronounced. The answer is yes. To J. I. W., a subtle "l" as in "meaL" tastes of potatoes, while a bolder "l" as in "Light" tastes of breakfast cereal.

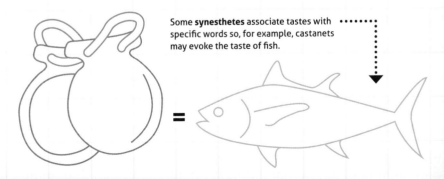

Some **synesthetes** associate tastes with specific words so, for example, castanets may evoke the taste of fish.

V. S. Ramachandran

Vilayanur S. Ramachandran, or "Rama" as he's affectionately known, is a behavioral neurologist renowned for his insights into the workings of the brain—many of which have come from the study of individual patients.

Program at the University of California, San Diego, as well as Adjunct Professor of Biology at the Salk Institute for Biological Studies, San Diego.

Ramachandran is brimming with energy and enthusiasm and is celebrated as much for his powers of communication as for his discoveries. In 2003 he became the first doctor or psychologist to give the BBC's Reith Lectures, which were subsequently published as the book *A Brief Tour of Human Consciousness*.

Born in India, Ramachandran was the son of a diplomat and raised all over the world. He originally trained as a doctor at Stanley Medical College in India before completing a Ph.D. in neurophysiology and experimental psychology at the University of Cambridge in England.

Today Ramachandran wears many hats, being both Director of the Center for Brain and Cognition and Professor in the Psychology Department and Neurosciences

His early work focused on vision and visual illusions. Such illusions, he has said, are like magic, and the joy of science is to find an explanation for that magic. Later on Ramachandran turned his attention to behavioral neurology and the study of patients with seemingly mysterious conditions. These include "phantom limb syndrome," in which sensations are still felt in a missing limb; anosognosia, in which patients with problems such as paralysis deny that there is anything wrong with them; and Capgras syndrome, in which patients believe their loved ones have been replaced by imposters. Ramachandran is also credited with reigniting research interest in synesthesia (pp. 24–25), and lately he has turned his attention to the search for universals in art, and to studying autism.

Phantom Limb Syndrome

Ramachandran was not the first person to document phantom limb syndrome, but his methods for studying the condition provide a good example of his Sherlock Holmes approach to science. For example, by using a pool cue to touch different parts of the body of a patient with phantom limb syndrome, Ramachandran was among the first to demonstrate the massive reorganization that is possible in the brain's sensory map of the body. When the patient was touched on his face, he reported experiencing a sensation in his missing hand.

This sounds bizarre, but it turns out that the brain's representations of the face and hand are next to each other. In the absence of feedback from the hand, the tissue representing the patient's face had invaded the now redundant tissue that previously served his missing hand. Ramachandran's playful attitude has also led him to propose

one of the few ways that exist to help people experiencing phantom limb pain. Such pain can come about if, for example, the patient has the sensation that their missing hand is clenched uncomfortably tight. Inspired by findings showing how visual input can overrule other sensory information (as shown with the rubber hand illusion on p. 19), Ramachandran devised a box with a mirror in the middle of it, perpendicular to the patient. If a patient inserts their healthy hand on one side of the mirror and places their damaged limb on the other side, the reflection in the mirror gives the impression that their missing hand has been resurrected. The patient can then uncurl the fingers of their healthy hand, so giving the appearance in the mirror that the fingers of their missing hand are also uncurling, in some cases leading to the alleviation of their phantom pain.

The patient puts their **healthy** hand and **damaged** hand into either side of the mirror box. The reflection tricks the brain into seeing two healthy hands

2.

Memory

Without memory we have no identity. We depend on it to remember who we are, where we've been, and to recognize the people who matter most to us. Contrary to the popular belief that memory is like a video recorder, we'll learn—through exercises and accounts of psychology studies—that it's actually a highly creative, unreliable process.

The Sea Slug

In many ways, memory is what makes us human. It provides our sense of identity, allows us to recognize the people we love, and to develop skills and learn about the world. Without memory, we'd be stuck in a Groundhog Day loop of endless reenactment. So why, when memory is so central to what it means to be human, does this chapter begin with a discussion of the sea slug?

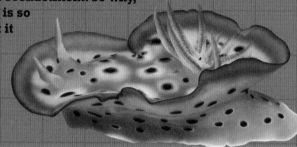

The sea slug has allowed scientists to study some of the most basic forms of memory. It has relatively few nerve cells—fewer than a million—many of which are quite large. In fact, some of the slug's nerve cells are up to a millimeter in diameter, in contrast to your own brain cells, which can be a hundred times narrower than that. Finally, the sea slug has easily identifiable nerve cells that can be studied in one individual creature, and then the same cell found and studied in another.

Habituation

Imagine you've bought a shiny new cellphone that keeps beeping every hour and you don't know how to stop it. At first the hourly chime is annoying, but gradually you become so used to it that you barely notice it

any more—you habituate to it. This is one of the forms of learning shown by the sea slug and studied by the Nobel Prize-winning scientist and memory pioneer Eric Kandel.

If you spray one of the sea slug's body parts, such as its gill, with seawater, it will withdraw the affected area from danger. But if you keep spraying, the slug will no longer show this withdrawal response because it will habituate to the sensation. Kandel studied in close detail the sensory neuron responsible for detecting the water spray, and the motor neuron that initiated the withdrawal response, to find out what was going on when the slug learned not to bother responding any longer.

Communicating Cells

He found first that the sensory neuron still responds to the repeated stimulation. By directly activating the motor neuron, he was further able to show that muscle fatigue was playing no part in the habituation process. This meant something must be going on in between—most likely related to the way nerve cells communicate with each other through the release of brain chemicals (neurotransmitters). Indeed, experiments suggested that habituation led to a reduced amount of neurotransmitter being released by the sensory neuron. Crucially, this ability for experience to change communication between nerve cells is thought to underpin our own ability to lay down new memories.

Sensitization

You're sitting quietly reading when the smoke alarm goes off, almost causing you to hit the ceiling. It was actually a false alarm, but knowing this doesn't stop you from feeling all jittery for the next few minutes. This ability for a powerful stimulus to put all our senses on edge is known as sensitization, and is another basic form of learning that Kandel studied in the sea slug. In this case, a noxious stimulus applied anywhere on the slug's body leaves its withdrawal response hyper-responsive for a length of time that depends on the strength of the earlier shock. Kandel's studies showed that whereas habituation is based on the sensory neuron releasing less neurotransmitter, sensitization seems to be caused by an "interneuron" affecting a given sensory neuron in such a way that it releases more neurotransmitter, thus leading to a heightened recoil response.

A sudden, unexpected noise may have you on the edge of your seat for a while.

How Much Can We Remember?

With some estimates suggesting that the human cortex contains upward of 10 billion neurons and each neuron making connections with 100,000 other neurons, there probably isn't any meaningful limit to how much information we can store away. Of course, whether or not we can recall that information when we want it is a whole other question. However, there is a kind of memory, known as short-term or "working" memory, which certainly does have limits and is more amenable to experimental measurement than long-term memory. Short-term memory is like your brain's desktop—it's what you use for holding information in mind for some purpose, such as when memorizing a telephone number before making a call.

TEST YOUR FRIENDS' SHORT-TERM MEMORY CAPACITY

A simple way to test working memory capacity is to read out a string of numbers of increasing length to your friends and see at what point they lose the ability to say the numbers back to you in the correct order. This is known as a digit-span task.

For example, start with just two numbers (4, 8) and wait for your friend to say them back. Then give them three

to recall (2, 5, 9) and keep going like that all the way up to... let's say a string of ten numbers. Of course you can get a friend to test you, too. What you'll probably find is that you and your friends are able to recall somewhere between five and nine numbers in the correct order. This is a robust finding in psychology research and was most famously discussed by George Miller in his groundbreaking paper "The Magical Number Seven, Plus or Minus Two."

CHUNKING

Things aren't quite so simple as they seem because the limit of seven, plus or minus two, applies to the number of meaningful chunks of information you're trying to recall, rather than the raw information. For example, we can recall approximately seven names, even though those names are made up of many more letters. You can test this out using the box below:

B	A	T	Y	Y
S	W	I	B	N
I	K	R	N	O
H	O	W	E	P
T	O	S	T	A

Try reading out the letters to a friend, starting from the bottom left-hand corner and working up each column in turn, beginning with just two letters at a time, then three at a time, and so on as you did earlier with numbers. At first, you might find your friend's memory is limited to around seven letters, as before. But if your friend is particularly shrewd they may start to recognize that the letters spell out a message that, once decoded, will make it easy for them to recall all 25 letters (This book was written by a pony). That's because once the message is decoded, the letters can then be understood as forming seven meaningful chunks.

Disrupting Short-Term Memory

....

Evidence indicates that we hold items in short-term memory by verbally rehearsing them silently in our mind—just think of how you say an unfamiliar phone number over and over to yourself before dialing. One way you can test out this idea is by repeating the short-term memory capacity tests on your friend—but this time get them to repeat an unrelated word out loud ("the," "the," "the") as they perform the task. You should find their memory performance suffers, presumably because the inner rehearsal process of their short-term memory has been compromised by their talking aloud.

Ways of Forgetting

In classic amnesia, the patient will probably know their name, have a reasonable sense of their life story, and will even be able to recall things, such as a phone number, over very short time periods. So far, so good, but ask them where they were yesterday or what they had for breakfast and they will look at you blankly. This is known as a deficit in episodic memory (or anterograde amnesia), and reflects an inability to lay down new long-lasting memories.

This kind of amnesia can have many causes such as a stroke or a bang to the head—for example, in a car crash. When this happens the patient will usually also suffer a loss of memory for events leading up to the crash, which is called retrograde amnesia. This period can be many years long, but often the memories will gradually return, beginning with the earliest, until a point near the moment of the crash, which will remain lost for ever.

Tales of Forgetfulness

The most famous amnesic is probably a patient known as H. M. He was an epilepsy sufferer whose seizures grew so bad that in the 1950s surgeons decided to remove a seahorse-shaped region called the hippocampus from both sides of his brain. Unfortunately, the surgeons at the time didn't realize the vital role played by the hippocampus, and after his operation H. M.'s memory was severely impaired, even though his personality and overall IQ remained relatively unaffected. However, one form of memory that remained intact in H. M., which is typical of amnesics, was his implicit memory. This meant he was able to learn new skills, such as puzzles or mazes, even though he would have no recollection of ever having seen them before.

An **amnesic** may tackle a puzzle but not remember seeing it before.

A famous anecdote of how implicit memory can remain intact in amnesics was told by Swiss psychologist Édouard Claparède. One day Claparède concealed a pin in his palm before shaking hands with an amnesic patient. The next day the same patient refused to take his hand, though she couldn't explain why.

Amnesics with intact **implicit memory** would refused to shake hands again if previously pricked with a pin.

THE CHAMELEON MAN

In the cases we've discussed so far, the amnesic patients have generally retained their sense of who they are. However, more rarely there are reports of patients who appear to have lost their identity.

In 2007, psychologists reported the real-life case of A. D., a 65-year-old whose identity appeared to be dependent on the environment he was in. His strange behavior began after a heart attack caused him to suffer damage to the fronto-temporal region of his brain. When he was with doctors, A. D. assumed the role of a doctor. When with psychologists he acted as though he were a psychologist, and when he was at the lawyer's... that's right, he claimed to be a lawyer. But apparently, A. D. didn't just say, "I am a doctor" or "I am a psychologist," he actually acted out the roles and provided plausible stories for how he came to be the character he believed he was.

A. D. maintained these assumed roles until the situation changed. The psychologists studying him said his condition was a mixture of a disinhibition syndrome—similar to utilization behavior, in which patients can't help themselves from using any objects or food in the vicinity— anterograde amnesia, and anosognosia, which is a lack of insight into one's disabilities or strange behavior.

However, there were limits to the roles A. D. would take on. For example, he didn't adopt the role of laundry worker at the hospital laundry, perhaps because it was rather beneath his real-life career as a politician!

Forgetting Faces

Most of us are remarkable face experts. Usually, all it takes is for us to meet someone once and their face seems to become embedded into our memory banks. We can even identify people from strange angles and in the most unhelpful lighting. However, there are some people for whom this expertise is lacking—they can't even recognize photographs of themselves. Their face blindness is known technically as prosopagnosia.

Historically, face blindness was considered to be extremely rare, resulting from brain damage caused by a stroke or an accident. But in the last few years, researchers have realized that many people are actually born with the condition.

Reasons for Forgetfulness

The fact that some people suffer face blindness after a specific part of their brain has been damaged has led some psychologists to suggest that we have a kind of dedicated "face processing" module. Supporting their argument is the finding that a specific area of the brain— the fusiform face area (FFA)—is activated strongly when we look at people's faces.

Other experts believe that our impressive ability with faces just happens to be particularly strong because we're exposed to people's faces every day. Supporting their argument is the fact that people who develop other forms of recognition expertise, such as the ability of bird watchers to distinguish between species, also show activation in the FFA, albeit to a lesser extent, when they look at birds.

IMPAIR YOUR FRIENDS' FACE RECOGNITION

Find photos of the faces of 28 strangers (not celebrities). Try cutting them out of magazines or printing them off the internet. Make sure the size of the photos is as similar as possible, and that only the face region is shown.

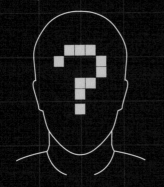

Now test as many friends as possible. Taking each friend in turn, present 14 of the faces to them, one at a time, for about three seconds each. You'll need to mark these 14 faces on the back, so that you can keep track of which faces you've shown and which you've kept behind.

After they've seen these 14 faces, get half your friends, to read for five minutes while the other half attempt a cryptic crossword—a task that's been found to disrupt people's memory for faces.

Next, mix up the original 14 faces with the remainder you didn't use, and then present all 28 of them,

one at a time, to your friends. Their task is to say whether each face was one of the ones shown to them earlier or not. Make sure you keep a score of your friends' accuracy, and leave about 30 seconds between the presentation of each face, during which time your friends must continue with their reading or cryptic crossword.

You should find that the scores of the friends who did the cryptic crossword are significantly less accurate than those who read. This replicates a study published by Cardiff-based psychologist Michael Lewis in the journal *Perception*.

According to his report, Lewis isn't sure why doing cryptic crosswords has this effect on face recognition, but he thinks a clue could come from the fact that so-called Navon stimuli also have this interfering effect. Navon stimuli are images in which a large letter or symbol is composed of many tiny repeats of a different letter or symbol. What cryptic crosswords and Navon stimuli may have in common is that they involve suppressing obvious, irrelevant information, which presumably has some kind of detrimental effect on the way our brains process faces. Lewis found that simple crosswords and Sudoku puzzles didn't have the same face-blinding effect.

Erasing Bad Memories

Memories of days such as 9/11 or even our first day at work, which take place under particularly emotional or stressful circumstances, tend to become etched into our brains and are known as "flash-bulb memories." This process makes sense from an evolutionary point of view— if we've been endangered or something happens that is of profound importance to our lives, it should help our future survival if we remember it well. The trouble is, the same process means that some people are unable to forget experiences that they'd rather leave behind.

The unwanted reliving of previous life-threatening experiences, in the form of flashbacks and nightmares, is today known as post-traumatic stress disorder (PTSD), which is also covered on pp. 120–121. By some estimates, 49 percent of rape victims experience PTSD and around 30 percent of bomb victims. During World War I, the same condition was referred to as shell shock. In fact descriptions of trauma-like symptoms date back to ancient Egyptian times.

Memory Blockers

Particularly threatening situations activate an almond-shaped structure found deep in the brain called the amygdala. This in turn leads to a rush of adrenaline and noradrenaline, which are thought to affect the processing of the seahorse-shaped hippocampus—a key brain area involved in human memory. The consequence is that we form a particularly long-lasting record of what happened, thus explaining the persistence of traumatic memories.

Greater understanding of these processes has prompted scientists to wonder if it might be possible to disrupt the forming of unpleasant memories, and so help prevent PTSD. Early findings seem to offer some hope. Psychiatrist Guillaume Vaiva and colleagues tested the effect of Propranolol, a beta-blocker that is taken by some cardiac patients. Propranolol binds to the same cell-surface receptors as adrenaline and noradrenaline. The theory is that it should be able to disrupt the formation of long-lasting traumatic memories by blocking the role played by these neurotransmitters.

Vaiva's team offered patients who arrived intact but shocked, either from car crashes or physical assault, the option to take Propranolol three times daily for the next seven days. Eleven patients agreed to this, while eight others declined but agreed to participate in the study. There was no difference in the severity of the trauma experienced by the two groups of patients, but when a psychiatrist assessed them two months later, he found PTSD symptoms were far lower in the group who took Propranolol.

Propranolol could even help reduce the impact of traumatic memories formed years ago. Research on mice has shown that when stressful memories are recalled there is a brief period during which they are vulnerable to unlearning, even if those memories were originally laid down a long time ago.

Inspired by this observation, in 2007 American psychiatrist Roger Pitman investigated what would happen if PTSD patients were given Propranolol after recalling their traumatic memories of events that had happened many years ago. A week later, when the patients listened to a recorded account of their traumatic experience, the patients previously given Propranolol suffered far less stress than those given a placebo.

Ethical Concerns

Most experts agree that it is just a matter of time before a reliable method of erasing unwanted memories is developed, but because of the ethical implications, not everyone believes this is good news. For example, what if the same methods are used to wipe the memories of witnesses to crimes? Or what will happen to the guiding influence of emotions like guilt, if a clear conscience is only a tablet away?

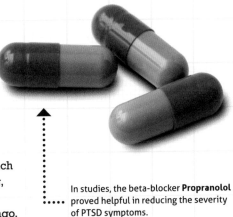

In studies, the beta-blocker **Propranolol** proved helpful in reducing the severity of PTSD symptoms.

Ten Ways to Boost Your Memory

Learn Mnemonics

When Eleanor Maguire and colleagues scanned the brains of ten world memory champions in 2003, they didn't find anything unusual about their brain structure or general IQ. However, during a memory task, the researchers found that brain areas related to movement and navigation were activated in the champs' brains, but not in the brains of ordinary folk. This probably reflects the way the champs used a mnemonic strategy called the "method of loci," which involves imagining items to be remembered (such as cards or numbers) as meaningful objects or people placed in various positions along a familiar route or journey.

Do Puzzles

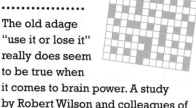

The old adage "use it or lose it" really does seem to be true when it comes to brain power. A study by Robert Wilson and colleagues of 801 nuns, priests, and monks over five years found that those who kept themselves busy with crosswords and games were less likely to develop Alzheimer's disease.

Wiggle Your Eyes

It sounds daft, but in 2007 Andrew Parker and Neil Dagnall reported that participants who wiggled their eyes from left to right after learning a list of words, subsequently remembered more of the words than participants who stared straight ahead or who wiggled their eyes up and down. The psychologists said moving the eyes from side to side can help the two brain hemispheres communicate with each other.

Summarize and Integrate

Summarizing the main points of what you've learned, and thinking deeply about how they relate to what you already knew and to your own experiences, leads to longer-lasting memories—a process known as "knowledge integration." One way to do this is to try to explain to your friends and family what you've just learned.

Sleep On It

A good night's sleep after learning is important if you want to consolidate your memories, but so too is having a solid snooze before you start studying. In 2007, Matthew Walker and colleagues found that sleep-deprived participants remembered 19 percent fewer pictures relative to controls who'd slept well. Brain scans showed less activity in the hippocampus of the sleep-deprived, a brain area responsible for laying down new memories.

Electrify Your Brain

When Canadian surgeons attempted to curtail the appetite of a dangerously obese man by stimulating an area deep in his brain called the hypothalamus, they were startled when he started recalling memories from decades earlier. Later tests showed that targeting the same area boosted his memory performance, and trials are now under way with Alzheimer's sufferers.

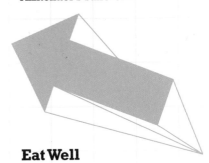

Eat Well

Especially when it comes to breakfast. Nutritionist Barbara Stewart reported in 2003 that children, especially girls, performed better on tests of attention and memory when they'd had beans on toast for breakfast, rather than just toast. Also, eat lots of fish—the "brain food" of choice. The fatty acids found in fish help prevent your brain from clogging up with trans-fats.

Pace Out Your Studies

Cramming doesn't work. The secret to remembering material in the long term is to review what you've studied periodically. Psychologists Doug Rohrer and Harold Pashler have conducted experiments showing that the optimum time after which you should review previously learned material is 10 to 30 percent of the total time for which you want to remember it. So if you're working toward an exam that's due in ten days' time, don't keep over-learning what you've studied; instead you're better off leaving the material and reviewing it a day later. If the exam is six months later, review the material after a month.

Feeling All Nostalgic

Ah, I remember it like it was only yesterday: My wife and I walking together along the Champs Élysées, the sun shining, birds singing away, traffic screeching past—those were the days. Sorry, I've gotten all nostalgic. We all do from time to time, but what is nostalgia and what purpose does it serve?

Nostalgia, from the Greek, means literally a return (*nostos*) of pain (*algos*), and indeed, doctors in the seventeenth and eighteenth centuries tended to think of nostalgia as a form of melancholy or even a neurological disorder. But today psychologists have a quite different view. Their experiments are showing that nostalgia can rescue us from misery when we're feeling down and lend meaning to our lives at times of existential crisis.

Nostalgic memories of happy times and places can be uplifting.

In a study by Tim Wildschut and colleagues, university students completed a measure of their loneliness, but with a twist. Afterward they were given false feedback, so that half of them were told they were much lonelier than the average student, and the other half were told they were much less lonely.

To reinforce the false feedback, the students were then asked to write about why they had scored the way they had.

After all this, the students completed a measure of nostalgia with some of the items being similar to those in the scale shown in the panel opposite. It turned out that the students who were tricked into believing they were lonely subsequently scored much higher on the nostalgia scale, supporting the psychologists' prediction that one role played by nostalgia is to comfort us from loneliness. Consistent with this, other research has shown that nostalgic thoughts often seem to feature other people.

HOW NOSTALGIC ARE YOU?

Below are responses reported to psychologists in studies of nostalgia.

1. I miss the way things were.

2. I sometimes reflect on bad things that have happened to me.

3. Overall there are more good things in my past than bad things.

4. I sometimes find myself thinking of the things I've missed out on in life.

5. Memories of happy times often pop into my mind.

6. I don't like thinking about the past because of bad things that have happened.

7. I sometimes reminisce fondly about my childhood.

8. I often think about vacations I've been on.

SCORING

Each time you answer "yes," a point is scored. Subtract any points for items 2, 4, and 6 from the total.

1 point or less: *Don't Look Back in Anger*—you're not at all nostalgic.

2-3 points: *Happy Days*—you're fairly nostalgic.

4-5 points: *Yesterday All My Troubles Seemed So Far Away*—you're always dreaming fondly of the past.

What's Your Earliest Memory?

If you're like most people, you won't be able to recall any memories from before you were about three and a half to four years old. Any memories from before this time appear to be lost for ever, thanks to what psychologists call "infantile amnesia." This gap in our memories is a bit of a mystery because two- and three-year-olds gladly talk about events from a year or so earlier in their lives, showing that memories from our very earliest years were at some point laid down in verbally accessible long-term memory.

In 2005 psychologist Carole Peterson and colleagues found that children younger than ten had earlier first memories (from when they were about three) than older children, but that after ten and up to adulthood there was no difference in the time of earliest memories, regardless of increasing age. The researchers said they had no idea what happens to our earlier memories when we pass the age of ten.

Elizabeth Loftus

Elizabeth Loftus has studied memory for nearly 40 years and is best known for her work showing the malleability of memory and the suggestibility of eyewitnesses. In the process she has received death threats and the highest awards obtainable, including in, 2005, the Grawemeyer Award for Psychology. In 2002 Loftus was listed as one of the top 100 most influential psychologists of the twentieth century by the *Review of General Psychology*—the highest-ranked woman on the list.

Loftus began her career by studying the way people classify animals and fruit, but soon decided she wanted her research to be more socially relevant. She's since consulted and testified in hundreds of criminal trials, including the case of Michael Jackson and the Bosnian War trials in the Hague. Today Loftus is a distinguished professor at the University of California, Irvine.

Some of Loftus's research has shown how easy it is to implant false memories in people's minds. For example, in one of her earliest studies, she and colleagues gave adult participants false feedback from relatives suggesting, alongside other truthful accounts, that they had had the experience of getting lost in a shopping mall as a child. The participants were asked to provide additional details of the incident if they could. A couple of weeks later, the participants were again asked about the shopping mall incident,

by which time many of them claimed to have memories of this fictitious event, in some cases even embellishing it with their own details.

Loftus demonstrated the power of **suggestion** by successfully feeding participants with false childhood memories of being lost.

Recovered Memory

In a more recent version of the study, Loftus and colleagues were able to put hundreds of undergraduate

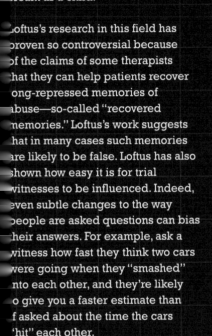

...udents on strawberry ice cream. All it took was false feedback from a computer program telling them about "that time" they were made sick by strawberry ice cream as a child.

Loftus's research in this field has proven so controversial because of the claims of some therapists that they can help patients recover long-repressed memories of abuse—so-called "recovered memories." Loftus's work suggests that in many cases such memories are likely to be false. Loftus has also shown how easy it is for trial witnesses to be influenced. Indeed, even subtle changes to the way people are asked questions can bias their answers. For example, ask a witness how fast they think two cars were going when they "smashed" into each other, and they're likely to give you a faster estimate than if asked about the time the cars "hit" each other.

"The truly horrifying idea is that what we think we know, what we believe with all our hearts, is not necessarily the truth."

—Loftus speaking to *Psychology Today* magazine, 1996

MANIPULATE YOUR FRIEND'S MEMORIES

First devise a list of between twenty and forty plausible life events that a person might have experienced as a child. Examples could include: "got into trouble for talking in class," "went to meet Santa Claus at a shopping mall," "had your tooth extracted at the dentist," and so on. Within that list, insert the following critical items: "broke a window with your hand," "had a lifeguard pull you out of the water," "got in trouble for calling 911."

Now find a willing friend and invite them to fill out this form, indicating which experiences they had as a child, and for each item get them to say how confident they are that they really had that experience. Afterward, ask them to use their imagination and spend four minutes thinking and writing about the four critical incidents, even if they're pretty sure they hadn't experienced them. Then leave the task for two weeks, and don't even mention it during that time.

Afterward, get your friend to complete the life-event list again, including rating their confidence in their memories for each item. If the experiment has worked, you will find this time around that your friend's confidence in their memory for the critical incidents has increased. This experiment shows how easy it is for us to confuse imagined events with real memories—part of the process that can lead to the generation of false memories.

3

Cognition

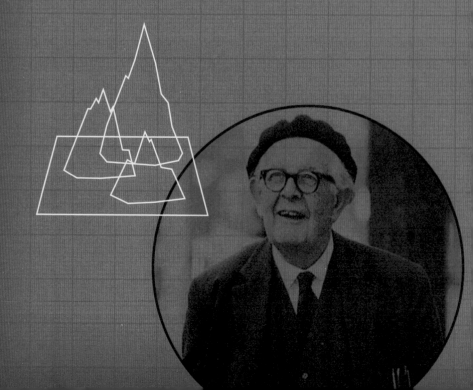

Early in the twentieth century, a branch of psychology known as behaviorism argued that we should only study outwardly observable behavior, leaving the workings of the mind as a black box. That all changed from the 1950s onward with the cognitive revolution, as psychologists focused ever more on the internal processes of the mind. This chapter is about those mental functions, including language, intelligence, decision-making, and number crunching.

Five Flaws in Your Thinking

We like to think of ourselves as rational beings, but in fact we're subject to numerous biases of egotism, self-deception, and wonky thinking. Five examples follow.

1. Stranger to Yourself

From unused gym memberships to broken promises to visit relatives, we're always committing ourselves to ventures that seem somehow less appealing once they arrive. It's almost as though our current selves, who make the arrangements, think our future selves are going to be so much more dedicated and patient. However, there is a positive side to this. Researchers have shown that we tend to underestimate our capacity to deal with unfortunate future events. When healthy people are asked to imagine the impact of a potential chronic illness on their mood, they see its likely effect as devastating. Yet when psychologists measured the mood of patients with end-state renal disease, requiring hemodialysis three times per week, it turned out they were just as happy as a group of healthy participants.

2. Unjustified Optimism

We underestimate our ability to cope with adverse events, but paradoxically we're also overly optimistic in that we think bad things are far more likely to happen to other people. A library's worth of studies have revealed the following anomalies: Students think they are less likely than average to suffer in their lifetime from a drinking problem or an early heart attack, or being fired from a job; smokers think they are less vulnerable than most to the ill effects of cigarettes.

3. You're More Generous to an Individual Than the Needy Masses

No doubt you consider yourself a fair person. And yet, if you're like the rest of us, a story of a single suffering individual pulls on your heartstrings far more forcefully than newspaper reports of a disaster affecting thousands. Think of how the world was gripped by the disappearance of the young British girl Madeleine McCann in Portugal, while elsewhere in the world many thousands of unidentified children go missing or are starved or killed every day.

Unfortunately, when psychologist Deborah Small tested what would happen to participants if they were educated about this bias, she found the discrepancy disappeared, not because participants donated more to the millions of starving people in Africa, but because they chose to give less to a single four-year-old girl whose plight they'd read about.

4. The "Power of One"

There's something about one unit or portion that we find appealing, a bias that Andrew Geier and colleagues at the University of Pennsylvania believe could underlie our irrational eating habits. In one study they left a bowl of M&M candies in the hallway of an apartment building with a sign saying "Help Yourself." How many sweets did people take? It depended on the size of the spoon left in the bowl—with people eating more if the spoon was bigger. Similarly,

measured by weight, significantly more pretzels were taken by passers-by when a complimentary bowl of 60 whole pretzels was left out, compared with a bowl of 120 half-pretzels.

You're likely to eat more **pretzels** if they're offered whole.

5. You're Wooed by Simple Names

Economists have been trying to predict share price fluctuations for years without success. The mistake they've made is to assume that people choose which shares to invest in on the basis of rational decisions. They'd have had more joy if they had appreciated the human tendency to favor easily processed information. Indeed, when Adam Alter and Daniel Oppenheimer at Princeton University analyzed real stock-market records, they found that, over a year, new shares in companies with easy-to-pronounce names tended to outperform shares in companies with more awkward names.

Issues of Intelligence

There are probably more definitions of intelligence than there are intelligence experts. In fact psychologists haven't even been able to agree on how many types of braininess there are.

Flavors of Intelligence

Early in the twentieth century, psychologist Charles Spearman proposed that there is really just one kind of intelligence, which he said explains why a person's performance on one form of intelligence test will predict their performance on a second. By contrast, psychologist Joy Guilford argued there are a whopping 120 different types. Howard Gardner of Harvard University believes there are between 7 and 9.5 forms of intelligence, including musical ability and kinesthetic skills.

Musical ability is considered to be a form of intelligence.

The Function of Intelligence

How can we discuss intelligence without agreement as to what it is, or whether it's a unitary concept? Most experts share the view that what we mean by intelligence is something to do with a person's capacity to learn and adapt. If a person is perceived to be intelligent by their culture, this is another way of saying that they have the tools needed to thrive in it; and, all other things being equal, they should therefore succeed in that environment relative to someone judged to be unintelligent. It follows from this that any meaningful measure of intelligence should have some predictive value.

Intelligence tests have been found to predict exam performance, work performance, and even mortality. Indeed, IQ tests predict work performance better than interviews, job references, and years in education. Intelligence-test performance also correlates with biological measures, such as brain size and reaction time, and to some extent it runs in families, lending further credence to the idea that something concrete and meaningful is being measured.

Are We Getting Cleverer?

Throughout the last century, each generation has tended to perform significantly better on tests of intelligence, suggesting that we are getting cleverer. The pattern, dubbed the "Flynn effect" after Professor James Flynn of the University of Otago in New Zealand, has been observed in every country that has long enough records.

However, Flynn argues that, rather than growing more intelligent, modern life and scientific progress have changed our style of thinking. In particular, he says we tend to see the similarities between things, whereas our ancestors were more interested in what things were useful for.

For example, asked what a dog and a rabbit have in common, we'd recognize them both as mammals, whereas an ancestor would recognize only that you use a dog to hunt rabbits. This argument is backed by a closer look at the parts of intelligence tests that we've collectively shown the greatest improvements on. We've demonstrated huge gains on the

"similarities" subscale of the Wechsler Intelligence Scale for Children, but only small gains on measures of verbal and general knowledge.

Disrupted Cognition

Classic neuropsychologists made many of their most important discoveries by studying patients with damage to specific parts of their brains. If a patient presented with a complaint such as a short-term memory problem, and it was later revealed at autopsy that they had suffered localized brain damage, then this would suggest, though by no means prove, that the afflicted brain area was somehow involved in short-term memory, and that the patient's preserved mental faculties were not dependent on the damaged brain area for their healthy functioning.

Compartmentalizing the Brain

Extending this line of reasoning, neuropsychologists have paid particular attention to cases where one patient has a deficit in one domain (say short-term memory) but not another (long-term memory), while a second patient has the reverse deficit—impaired long-term memory, but intact short-term memory. This "double-dissociation" provides powerful evidence that the two faculties operate independently of each other. If the two patients also have differing patterns of brain damage, further strong inferences can be made about the neuroanatomical basis of the mental domains in question.

One of the most famous examples of this kind of approach to psychology comes from the work of the French surgeon Paul Broca and the German neurologist Carl Wernicke in the nineteenth century. Broca reported the case of a patient with localized damage to the rear part of his left frontal lobe, whose comprehension was intact, but who could only utter the syllable "tan," hence his nickname "Tan-tan." By contrast, Wernicke described a syndrome following damage to the temporal lobe, which left patients able to produce speech, but with their comprehension devastated, with the consequence that what they said was often garbled nonsense. Taken together, these observations show that the brain handles comprehension and the production of speech separately.

Don't Try This at Home

Today psychologists can mimic this approach by using a hand-held magnet to temporarily disrupt activity in a localized area of a volunteer's brain. The technique is known as "transcranial magnetic stimulation" (TMS). Holding a pulsing magnet over a volunteer's head induces a rapidly changing magnetic field in the neural tissue beneath, thus altering the electrical communication between brain cells. Stimulation at low frequency generally inhibits brain activity, while higher frequencies increase brain activity in the affected region.

This man is undergoing **transcranial magnetic stimulation (TMS)**, a method that stimulates small areas of the brain.

A key advantage of the technique is that if knocking out a given brain area results in some behavioral effect, researchers can then conclude confidently that the affected brain region is "necessary" for that behavioral function. By contrast, when brain scanning reveals that a given brain region is active during a particular behavioral task, researchers can only conclude that the activity and the function are correlated—they can't infer any causal relation between the two.

SO WHAT WAS PHRENOLOGY?

The phrenologists of the eighteenth and nineteenth centuries shared with more modern thinking the view that the mind is rooted in the brain. However, whereas modern-day psychologists consider different mental processes to be carried out by localized brain areas, the phrenologists wrongly argued that entire personality traits were somehow localized to a certain brain area, and that they could be read via bumps on the skull. At the height of its popularity, phrenology boasted many societies around the world dedicated to its study. Today, some skeptical commentators believe the localization of function or "blobs on the brain" approach to psychology has gone too far, and accuse their brain-imaging colleagues of being like modern-day phrenologists.

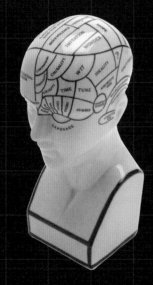

Speaking of Thoughts

Can we think about things for which we lack the relevant words? In the first half of the twentieth century, the linguist Edward Sapir and his student Benjamin Whorf argued that we can't—that language constrains thought—and today their views are known as the Sapir–Whorf hypothesis.

Sapir and Whorf's ideas are probably best illustrated by the urban myth that claims because Inuits have numerous words for snow, they are able to distinguish between many different categories of the fluffy stuff. By contrast, to speakers of other languages, such as English, which have only one word for snow, snow is, well, just snow.

The evidence is conflicting. An example of how language affects thought comes from studies of the 200-strong Pirah tribe in the Amazon, who have just two numerical words: "hói" with an accent and "hoi," without, signifying "one" and "two." Any quantities above two they simply refer to as "many."

American psychologist Peter Gordon tested the Pirah on a number of numerical matching tasks. For example, he placed a number of batteries in a row and asked the Pirah to lay out the same number. When there were one, two, or three batteries, the tribespeople performed fine, but after that, the greater the number of batteries, the less accurate they became. The tests appeared to show that the tribe was unable to think about numbers for which they lacked the words.

On the other hand, Professor Stanislas Dehaene and his colleagues at the Collège de France in Paris have found evidence that humans are capable of thinking about concepts for which they lack

the words. Dehaene's team studied another Amazonian tribe, the Munduruku, and found that they were able to solve geometric problems and make use of a map even though they have no words for describing spatial relations.

The Strange Case of the Language Switchers

It's amazing that people who speak fluently in two languages or more are able to stay focused on one language at a time, without flitting back and forth between the two. One theory for how they do this suggests a kind of switch at the front of the brain, which acts as a language controller. Support for the idea comes from reports by Kuan Kho and colleagues of two patients who underwent brain surgery as part of their treatment for epilepsy.

One Dutch–English bilingual had half his brain anesthetized, which seemed to flip his switch over to the English position. Attempting to recall a story told to him earlier, he was only able to do so in English. Any Dutch he spoke, he pronounced with an English accent. Then there was the French–Chinese bilingual. His surgeons asked him to count aloud as they prodded his brain with an electrode in an attempt to locate the neural tissue involved in language. He started in French, but then as he reached seven, the surgeons moved their prodding to the front of his left hemisphere, at which point he involuntarily switched to Chinese.

The Pirah tribespeople struggle with number calculations as they only have a numerical vocabulary for the words "one," "two," and "many."

Dyslexia

....

Dyslexia, from the Greek, means literally a difficulty with words. The first description of the condition is often attributed to the English family doctor W. Pringle Morgan, who reported in 1896 on the case of a 14-year-old boy with "word blindness." The boy was said to be bright and intelligent, yet he struggled to read. Today, dyslexia is thought to affect at least 5 percent of the population. It runs in families, which suggests it has a strong genetic component, and it is often associated with secondary symptoms, such as a difficulty in telling left from right, or postural instability.

A hallmark of the condition is that people with dyslexia struggle with the sounds, known as phonemes, that make up words. If I asked a non-dyslexic to pronounce a nonsense word like "Bagadiboo," they wouldn't have a problem, because they would translate the letters of the word into their appropriate sounds. By contrast, a person with dyslexia would have great difficulty with this.

However, the diagnosis of dyslexia is not quite as straightforward as it might seem. A popular view is that a level of reading ability that is low relative to the child's overall intelligence characterizes dyslexia. Yet "bad readers" of low general intelligence make the same kind of reading errors, and have the same difficulty with word sounds, as do children with dyslexia. Moreover, dyslexic children and other "bad readers" benefit in the same way from the same kind of interventions, which has led some experts to argue that the concept of dyslexia is meaningless.

The most mainstream treatments for dyslexia place great emphasis on teaching children what are known as phonological skills, to help them learn to process the sounds that words are made of. Other, more controversial treatments tend to focus on the possible causes of the dyslexic child's difficulties. For example, some experts think that a subset of children with dyslexia have difficulty reading black print on a white background, and so they prescribe colored lenses to help with this. Other experts have linked dyslexia with an abnormality in a part of the brain known as the cerebellum, which is involved with movement control. This theory has led to exercise-based treatments.

Acquired Dyslexia

Some people develop dyslexia after suffering brain damage. When this happens, the patient will usually have one of three types of dyslexia. Phonological dyslexia is a problem with translating letters into sounds, of the kind typically seen in children with dyslexia. So-called "surface dyslexia" is the opposite problem. In this case the patient can translate letters into sounds, but they can't read words whole. This means they can't read irregular words like "pneumonia," which have to be processed whole. Then there's "deep dyslexia," which relates more to a problem with the meaning of words. A patient with this condition might read the word "bus" as "tram" because they will have muddled the two related meanings.

The Boy with Hyperlexia

While children with dyslexia struggle to read, often in spite of having normal intelligence, psychologists in 2006 documented the contrasting case of a four-year-old autistic boy who struggled with most mental tasks except reading. In fact, he was a scarily good reader, even able to pronounce unusual words such as "yacht." According to his mother, the boy started looking through newspapers with zeal before he was even two. Keith Atkin and Marjorie Lorch who documented the case said current accounts of how children learn to read cannot explain this child's literacy abilities. However, they did add that because of his communication difficulties it was unclear how much he understood of what he read.

A child with **hyperlexia** will have a reading ability way above the average for their age.

Jean Piaget

Born in 1896 in Neuchâtel, Switzerland, Jean Piaget would become one of the most influential thinkers of the twentieth century, and the most highly cited psychologist after Sigmund Freud. He is credited with founding the field of genetic epistemology—the study of how knowledge develops. After a career in which he published 75 books and hundreds of academic papers, his influence on developmental psychology and educational practice is still felt strongly today.

Piaget was a child prodigy who published his first journal paper at just 11 years old, entitled "On Sighting an Albino Sparrow." In 1918 his study of mollusks led to the award of a doctorate, after which he traveled to Zurich to work with the psychoanalyst Carl Jung. In 1919 he was invited to work in the laboratory of Alfred Binet in Paris, calculating the average intelligence-test performance of children at different ages—here he became fascinated by the mistakes that children make.

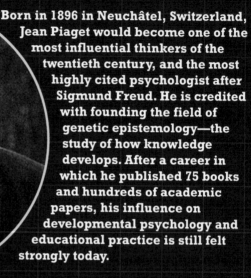

In 1923 Piaget married Valentine Châtenay and together they studied their three children. From observing the kind of errors children make, Piaget concluded that they think in a profoundly different way from adults. He believed that children acquire their knowledge about the world by interacting with it; and crucially, he thought their understanding of the world advanced in discrete, qualitative stages, such that a child in an earlier stage would be incapable of grasping a concept that required his or her advancement to a later stage.

In 1955 Piaget established the International Center for Genetic Epistemology in Geneva and acted as its director until his death in 1980. Piaget was obsessed with his work. He wrote every morning, even when traveling abroad for lectures.

The four stages that Piaget believed all children advance through were known as the sensorimotor stage (birth to about two years), the pre-operational stage (from two to seven years), the concrete operational stage (from seven to twelve years), and the formal operational stage. Piaget believed the stage a child is at can be revealed by the errors they make in his famous tasks, such as the "Three-Mountain Task" and his conservation problems.

In some cases, more modern research is showing that the errors children make are not caused by their lack of conceptual understanding, but rather by the limitations of their physical coordination. For example, Piaget believed young children are unable to think about objects that they can't see. But the reason infants don't reach for such objects may be because they're not capable of reaching around an obstacle, not because they think the object doesn't exist once it is out of sight.

The Three-Mountain Task
....

Piaget created a three-dimensional model of the Genevan mountain Le Salève and two other surrounding peaks. Children were asked to sit in front of the model and try to imagine the view from different perspectives. They might be asked to choose a photo that showed the mountains

from a different angle to their own. Children younger than four don't understand what is being asked of them. Children between four and six understand what's asked of them but are unable to take another person's perspective in this way—thus demonstrating what Piaget called their egocentrism.

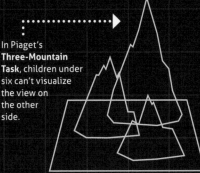

In Piaget's **Three-Mountain Task**, children under six can't visualize the view on the other side.

Conservation Problems
....

Pre-school children are unable to grasp that superficial changes in the appearance of matter don't affect its basic properties. For example, if you pour liquid from a short stubby glass into a tall thin one, a watching preschooler will likely say there is more liquid in the second glass simply because the level is higher. Similarly, if you spread out counters on a table, the young child will mistakenly think they must have grown in number.

Creativity

Creativity isn't just about composing a groovy tune or painting a sublime landscape—it's also about breaking new ground and considering problems in innovative and useful ways. After all, where would human civilization be today if people had always accepted the status quo?

Creativity tends to work in three stages: there's the preparation stage, which involves studying a problem from as many different angles as possible. Next is the incubation period. Novel ideas rarely arrive on demand. In fact, they often come once you've stopped thinking about a problem deliberately, and your unconscious mind has had time to work behind the scenes. The third and final stage is the "Aha!" or "Eureka" moment of insight.

It is usually the Eureka moment that we read about in biographies or interviews, which gives rise to the popular illusion of effortless creativity. Nobel Prize winning Kary Mullis said his idea for the polymerase chain reaction, an innovation that has revolutionized biological research, came to him suddenly while driving. Michael Jackson said that many of his classic hits fell into his lap, as if they were a gift from God.

The ultimate Renaissance man, **Leonardo da Vinci (1452–1519)** is renowned for his genius and prolific creativity. He was a brilliant artist, scientist, architect, engineer, and inventor.

Who Can Be Creative?

A myth that deserves debunking is the idea that some people are capable of being creative while others aren't. Anyone can be creative and creativity can be nurtured. That said, creative types do tend to show certain characteristics.

Intelligence usually plays a part but it is not sufficient for attaining creativity. In fact, extremely high scorers on intelligence tests tend to lack creativity, probably because they have mastered a convergent style of thinking that leads them to zoom in on the right answer, whereas creativity depends on a divergent thinking style—often referred to as lateral thinking, or "thinking outside the box."

Creative people tend to be curious and inquisitive. We all have to filter out irrelevant information, otherwise we'd be swamped by data overload, but research shows creative characters have less strict filters. This could help explain the observed association between creativity and psychosis. Some experts have argued that a flexible thinking style combined with an openness to sensory experience can lead to creativity when successfully channeled, but to mental illness if it becomes overwhelming.

Another myth is that creative people are lazy, tending to lie back and wait for big ideas to hit them. The truth is the opposite. Creative people tend to be extremely well read and informed on the topics that interest them. Creativity is about bringing ideas together in new ways, so the more raw material that is available to a thinker, the more likely they are to come up with a novel and useful idea.

The Neuroscience of Creativity

Mounting evidence suggests that the kind of divergent thinking required for creativity is handled largely by the right hemisphere of the brain. Patients with a rare type of dementia known as fronto-temporal dementia, which particularly affects the left hemisphere, often show enhanced creativity. It's as though their right hemisphere has been released from suppressive supervision by the more logical, literal left hemisphere.

Supporting this account are studies by Edward Bowden and colleagues showing that solutions reached via creative insight are associated with increased activity in the right hemisphere. Moreover, people can more quickly find solutions to problems they weren't able to solve, when they are presented in their left visual field (processed by the right hemisphere) as opposed to their right visual field. This suggests the right hemisphere was closer to reaching the answer than the left hemisphere was.

Number Blindness

In the same way that some people have a problem with reading, often out of keeping with their overall intelligence, others appear to have a specific deficit when it comes to even the most simple acts of mental arithmetic. People with number blindness or dyslexia/dyscalculia, as it's known, struggle to answer 5 + 2. Some might even have difficulty if you asked them to say whether the answer is in the ballpark of say 40 or 50—they lack that gut feeling of numerical size that most of us take for granted.

Meaning literally to "count badly," from the Greek, dyscalculia is thought to affect around 5 percent of the population, yet is barely heard of relative to its better-known cousin dyslexia. A skill that is often found to be lacking in people with dyscalculia is known as subitizing—the ability to grasp in an instant, without the need for counting, how many items there are in a group of four or fewer.

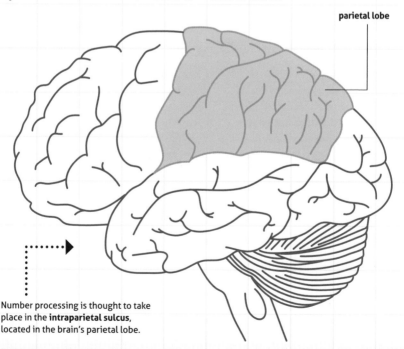

parietal lobe

Number processing is thought to take place in the **intraparietal sulcus**, located in the brain's parietal lobe.

Brain-imaging studies carried out in the last few years have revealed that children with dyscalculia have structural and functional abnormalities in a part of the brain called the intraparietal sulcus—a region in the parietal lobe, toward the rear of the head, which probably acts as a kind of number-processing module.

This idea was backed up by a transcranial magnetic stimulation (TMS) study in 2007 that involved presenting "normal" participants and dyscalculics with numbers that differed in their physical size (how BIG they were written), their numerical size, or both. The participants' task was to say in each case which was the bigger of the two numbers, based on physical or numerical size, depending on the trial. The "normal" participants found the task easier when both the physical size and numerical size of each number were equal. However, when TMS was applied to their intraparietal sulcus, thus temporarily interfering with processing in that region, they no longer benefited from the numerical and physical size of each number being the same—that is, their performance resembled that of the dyscalculics.

Is There Really a Mental Number Line?

Psychologists and philosophers have long held the belief that when we think about numbers we refer to a mental number line, stretching from lower numbers at one end to higher numbers at the other. For years the idea seemed difficult to test, but in 1993 Stanislas Dehaene and colleagues asked people to respond with their right or left hand according to whether a digit was odd or even. A key pattern to emerge was that the participants were quicker to respond to larger numbers with their right hand and to smaller numbers with their left hand. The researchers argued that this was because responding to a larger number is easier with the right hand, as the number is represented mentally toward the right of an imaginary number line, and vice versa for small numbers—an effect they dubbed the "Spatial Numerical Association of Response Codes effect" or SNARC.

A number line provides a simple visual aid to help with numerical ordering and calculations.

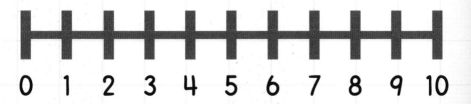

4

Affect

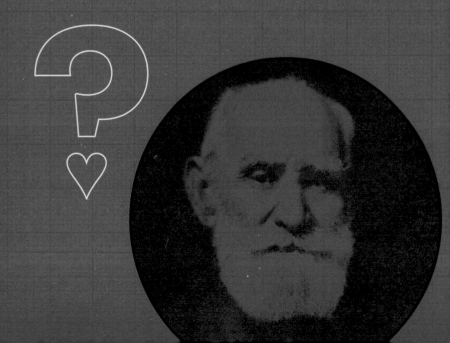

All can be going swimmingly in life and yet for some people a dark cloud of misery lingers. Meanwhile others seem to enjoy a sunny outlook, no matter the obstacles life throws in their path. This chapter is about our emotional lives, and how our thinking styles and habits affect the way we feel.

How Emotions Affect Us: Part 1

· · · · · · · · · · · · · · · · · · ·

Have you ever had a "good hair day" on a day when you were depressed? It's not likely. More often, the day when you're late for school is the same day you forget your homework, you argue with your parents, and so on... How many times have we said to ourselves, "Why can't something good just happen when I really need it to?" Neuroscience, unfortunately, doesn't wire us to work this way. The term "state of mind" emerges from the realities of how our brain works...

The next time you notice that you are in an especially good mood, make a list of all the things that have gone right for you lately, all the things you are happy about. The chances are that your positive frame of mind will generate a long list of great things. Then, the next time you are feeling especially negative or cranky, repeat this exercise. Now, it is more likely that the list will be harder to create a second time.

The Meaning of Moods

· ·

The reason that we can see the good in everything when we are happy, but only the bad side of things when we are upset or angry is that individual emotions feed into the longer-term state of mind commonly called a mood. Also, alongside these psychological factors that influence your mood, are biological ones such as health, diet, and biorhythms.

Our present mood affects which other memories are most readily accessible—known as mood-dependent memory—so that when we are in a good mood, we might recall good memories, and vice versa. Thinking about a lost loved one, for example, evokes sadness and this can trigger other sad memories. Suddenly we're thinking about the ended romance, the failed exam, and so on.

What Can You Do?

Knowing that emotion creates mood helps combat the idea that our current thoughts are our one and only reality. Psychologist Robert Thayer also recommends "a combination of relaxation, stress management, cognitive control, and exercise," to improve your mood.

Time out stroking a pet can have a significant calming effect on your mind.

THE DURABILITY BIAS—
A THOUGHT EXPERIMENT

So, does the fact that our emotions are not set responses to particular triggers mean we are all at the mercy of our moods? If something bad happens, do we run the risk of spiraling into depression? Predict how long you might anticipate feeling bad if the following events occurred:

(a) Your team lost the championship.
(b) You broke up with your girlfriend.
(c) You failed a test.

Researchers have found that when people predict how long they will feel bad after a negatively perceived event, they overestimate the duration of the emotional impact. Whatever our emotions, although we have ups and downs, we tend to

return to a neutral "home" position within a relatively short period of time. This effect is referred to as the durability bias.

The inaccuracy of our predictions is linked to our tendency to be overly focused on the here and now, and the concepts of alternate future possibilities tend not to enter our minds. People who tend to show greater flexibility and adaptability in their views and think of alternate possibilities as exciting also report greater levels of enjoyment. However, the greater the disruption to the neutral emotion, and the more often a person stays in the negative processing state, the more difficult it can be for them to return to a balanced state of perception.

How Emotions Affect Us: Part 2

. . . .

The way emotions affect us is key to our understanding of psychology. However, these theories have changed over the years—even though the ideas of Freud's ego, id, and superego or terms such as "repression" or "Oedipus complex" are still part of a general mainstream body of knowledge. A brief summary of this progression follows.

There are various theories on the cause of "maladaptive behavior" (dysfunctional behavior aimed at reducing anxiety). Psychodynamic theorists agree that human behavior is largely motivated by unconscious processes. In these theories, there is an assumption of a set of universal principles that explain personality development and behavior. Development early in the lifespan has a profound effect on the adult one becomes, and gaining insight into the unconscious conflict is a large component of psychotherapy.

For Sigmund Freud, maladaptive behavior was the result of an unconscious unresolved conflict that occurred during childhood. He believed that anxiety is the basis of all neuroses, and maladaptive "defense mechanisms" are faulty ways in which the personality tries to avoid the anxiety experience. For Freud, personality is dictated on the basis of biological drives and the inner conflict is a result of

modulating biological drives. With time, theorists began to disagree with Freud's ideas, instead attributing behavior and personality traits to the influences of society, relationships, and free will.

Ensuing movements in psychology emerged that focused largely on the "here and now" of experience. Some theorists believe it is not at all necessary to understand the "whys" of how things got to be this way for a person to be able to change the maladaptive behavior, but instead emphasize developing solutions and focusing on motivation.

The Behaviorists

. . . .

Some approaches to therapy focus completely on achieving specific changes in behavior. Classic and operant conditioning are well-known examples of behavioral modification theory. Within classical conditioning, Nobel Prize winning physiologist Ivan Pavlov's experiments with dogs showed that after a bell was consistently paired with food, dogs would salivate upon hearing the bell, even when no food was present.

Pavlov's dogs salivated whenever the bell was rung—whether he brought them food or not.

Operant conditioning, most associated with B. F. Skinner, associates behavioral conditioning with stimuli that are learned instead of innate reactions (as is a salivation response to food). For example, if a woman visits hospital and the experience provokes anxiety, subsequent visits to the hospital may also arouse anxiety, even for an innocuous event such as visiting a friend there who had given birth.

Treatment through behavioral modification is widely applied in the treatment of phobias and anxiety disorders, and is quite regularly utilized in resolving behavioral difficulties with children. The use, for example, of a "token economy" where a child receives a star or other reward to enforce proper behavior is an example of behavioral modification through operant conditioning, pairing environmental stimuli to reinforce desired behavioral results.

Systematic desensitization is an approach based on classical conditioning theory most commonly used to treat anxiety disorders. Gradually more intensive and repeated exposure to an anxiety-provoking stimulus (using real or guided imagery) is paired with relaxation training in a safe environment. The stimulus is paired with the experience of nondisastrous results when exposure to the imagined danger does not occur, gradually extinguishing the anxiety response.

Cognitive Behavior

The most common approach to psychotherapeutic treatment is that of cognitive behavioral therapy (CBT). This treatment emerged out of growing dissatisfaction with what seemed to be shortsightedness of parts of both the behavioral and the psychodynamic models. CBT combines the roles that cognitive factors play in shaping behavior in these theories. These approaches examine patterns of mistaken belief and irrational thought, and their effect on a person's misguided emotional state, and resulting behavior.

Emotion in the Brain

Emotions are the most guiding and pervasive force behind individual psychology. They influence our decisions, our ideas of right and wrong, our relationships, the health of our bodies, and they influence our perceptions from the most subtle areas of our lives to the most all-consuming. Indeed, it would be nearly impossible to find a sphere of cognition immune to the influence of emotions.

But what are emotions? Where do they come from? Can we control them, or do they control us? Are emotions a matter of perception? Do we have the power to change our emotions, and thereby change our thoughts and our experience? Or must we begin by changing our thoughts, and thereby change our emotional state?

THE THOUGHT-EXPERIENCE CONNECTION

True or False?

1. A lovers' quarrel can delay the healing of a wound.

2. When a patient believes that something he or she is given will relieve pain, the body actually releases the pain-killing endorphins even when a placebo is administered.

3. One bad thing happening neurologically codes how our brain will rank other unrelated events and perceptions.

4. Under clinical hypnosis, someone who is told he or she is being touched by a burning-hot object can produce a blood blister when actually touched by an object at room temperature.

•••••••••••••••••••••••••••••••••••••••

ANSWERS

Amazingly these are all true. The connection between thoughts and experiences is so strong it has physical effects.

Making Emotions Real

Can you think of a time when a coach told you to visualize yourself hitting the home run before a big game, when a friend "talked you out of a bad mood," or when you aced a test because you "knew" you could do it? The scientific reality is that our bodies respond to mental input as if it were physically real—images create bodily responses just as if the experiential stimuli have occurred.

Electrocardiogram measurements in a number of studies, including those by Erfani and Efanian, show that mental rehearsal sends the same messages to your brain as when you are actually doing the real exercise. The implications of these realities are astounding. Scientists have a good understanding of the neurological systems behind emotion and feelings. Dopamine is associated with experiencing pleasure, happiness, and reward, low serotonin is implicated in depression, and endorphins are produced and released in the brain after exercise, sex, eating chocolate, viewing beautiful art, watching a touching dramatic scene, or even listening to an evocative piece of music. The fact that training our thinking mechanisms can guide physiological processes allows ourselves greater responsibility for actions relating to our own success and well-being.

When a tennis player is fully focused on the ball, they are said to be "**in the zone**."

Positive Psychology

Positive psychology encourages people to focus their daily lives on getting the most rewarding experiences, by learning to manage the daily rhythms of life. By being able to concentrate on these rhythms, a person can achieve a sense of "flow"—a concept described by Hungarian psychologist Mihály Csíkszentmihályi—in which goals are challenging but achievable, and a person's actions are focused but apparently effortless. It is a concept that is perhaps most often described in relation to sports stars, who, after a particularly good performance, claim to have been "in the zone."

Facial Recognition

Sono felice di vederli. Je suis heureux de vous voir. Eu sou feliz vê-lo. **I am happy to see you. Italy, France, Portugal, and Britain exist in relatively close geographical proximity to one another, but if we relied solely on language to convey the above message, it is obvious how difficult things would be.**

Fortunately, we determine much of what another person is feeling from the expression on their face. The feelings most often expressed in both literate and preliterate societies are universal in their facial language of communication: anger, disgust, fear, and happiness. But advanced communication and interpretation of emotions requires more than simply the processing of a person's facial expression, and calls for us to take in to account other factors, creating a bigger picture. We smile when we are happy, but also when we're embarrassed or even resigned. Vocal speed and tone, background, and other personality data are all interwoven in recognition. How does the brain recognize and translate these levels of information to communicate emotionality?

Our facial expressions communicate a lot about how we are feeling.

Research has shown that visual sensory input (in this case, the facial expression) is initially processed by coding spatial relation and configuration. It is impossible to determine "angry" eyebrows or an "angry" mouth in isolation from the rest of the face. For example, angry eyebrows may appear the same as perplexed eyebrows, so a different mouth position may differentiate the two. At the next level of processing, additional stimulus recognition occurs, and things can be classified or placed as belonging to a familiar perceptual category. Semantic processing then occurs, where meaning can be drawn from associations with past experiences, emotions evoked in one's self, context, and background. Finally, naming processes are activated and retrieved ("smile").

Empathy

The fact that an emotion in another tends to evoke a similar emotion in oneself further helps us categorize the stimuli and "understand" the emotions of one another. In experiential terms, the ramifications of this are complicated. This helps us to understand further why a bad mood can be contagious, and why spending time with less than emotionally healthy people can be dangerous for one's own mental health.

▲ Can you tell if this person is **cross** or **confused**?

Studies show that the truth behind the old saying "Misery loves company" is more accurately "Misery loves miserable company." When given the choice to be alone or with others, depressed people chose first to be in the company of other similarly struggling people, or secondly to be alone. They did not choose to be around people who were not likewise depressed.

It has been found that people respond more quickly toward those stimuli that evoke positive emotions than stimuli that evoke negative emotions. If that isn't firm evidence that the best way to get through to someone is not through intimidation or expressing anger, then what is?

Our ability to understand others may literally lie in our ability to understand ourselves, and also in our shared experiences. Interesting examples of this can be found in studies of subjects who had suffered brain damage that left them unable to experience specific emotions. For example, in a study undertaken by British neuropsychologist Andy Calder and colleagues, subjects suffering from Huntington's disease who were unable to experience disgust also had trouble recognizing facial expressions of disgust.

Depressing Cognitive Distortions

AN INVENTORY FOR YOUR LIFE

	strongly disagree	disagree	neutral feelings	agree	strongly agree
I have a likeable personality.	☐	☐	☐	☐	☐
I have much to offer to a significant other.	☐	☐	☐	☐	☐
I have intimate, strong, and equal relationships.	☐	☐	☐	☐	☐
I am able to communicate and get my needs met.	☐	☐	☐	☐	☐
I can accept failure in myself and others.	☐	☐	☐	☐	☐
My friends can depend on me.	☐	☐	☐	☐	☐
I can depend on my friends.	☐	☐	☐	☐	☐
I am satisfied with my life.	☐	☐	☐	☐	☐
I am satisfied with myself.	☐	☐	☐	☐	☐
I am satisfied with how others treat me.	☐	☐	☐	☐	☐
I am able to handle difficulties.	☐	☐	☐	☐	☐
I have found opportunities that suit me.	☐	☐	☐	☐	☐
I am able to make the best out of a situation. When mistakes happen, I am more concerned with figuring out how to fix it than needing to know whose fault it is.	☐	☐	☐	☐	☐

As we have established, there are patterns in thinking and perception that influence one's overall levels of happiness. The exercise to the left is meant to serve as a guide to explore some of your own tendencies. Review your answers. Are they clustered in any one area? What can this tell you about yourself?

Psychotherapists sometimes use such inventories in order to reveal potential depressing cognitive distortions that certain personality types may get trapped in. Here are a couple of the most common ones:

Learned Helplessness
....

One of the most depressing cognitive distortions is that of "learned helplessness," a concept introduced in the late 1960s by Martin Seligman. In a state of learned helplessness a person believes themselves to be stuck in a situation over which they have no control, and that any efforts to improve that situation are futile—so no such attempts are made. However, this sense of helplessness is rarely accurate. Those people with such a perception tend to take little responsibility for their own decisions, may not feel respected, and may hesitate to demand that respect. It may also be difficult for them to express or communicate their inner experiences, and they may feel isolated and that "the world is against them." However, by understanding the nature of the distortion from which they suffer, a person may feel empowered to make some changes, and happiness can often be just a few steps away.

Perfectionism
....

The pursuit of perfection, for some of us, can render us incapable of enjoying our lives. While a person with a well-balanced personality can accept that he or she may be better at certain things than others, and may derive satisfaction from doing something well, a neurotic perfectionist—as described by Don Hamachek—may in their own mind "never seem to do things good enough to warrant that feeling [of satisfaction]."

The risks associated with perfectionism are many, and it can be an indicator of a number of other problems such as obsessive-compulsive disorder (pp. 104–105).

Perfectionism is a dangerous distortion: nothing is ever enough, and nothing is ever good enough. Being patient with ourselves and our lives, and letting where we are and what we have simply be enough, is one of the most important skills to master in the art of achieving happiness.

Why Do We Love Who We Love?

Love has to be blind. In the first stage of falling in love, we idealize our partner. In our mind's eye, we amplify the traits that we are drawn to and focus on what we want to see. We choose to ignore, dismiss, or underemphasize the traits we don't like. This is furthered by the tendency for each of us to "be at our best" at the beginning of the relationship, something for which we then often credit our beloved—how ironic! The majority of new couples also think their relationship is "special" when compared to others, and that they have found something deeper and more intimate than what other couples share. This blind love may serve to allow us to progress to the stages where the following chemistry begins.

WHO DO YOU LOVE?

Research has shown who we fall for.

Love yourself? We tend to fall for someone who looks like we do.

Love your daddy? We tend to fall for someone who looks like our parents.

Dr. Martha McClintock at the University of Chicago has carried out studies that show we are also attracted to people who have complementary immune systems to ours, something we subconsciously determine through each other's odor.

At the University of California Albert Mehrabian has also suggested that we assign likeability to others in surprising ways. According to his studies, words play a relatively minor part, and instead some 55 percent of whether we find someone appealing can be attributed to body language, 38 percent to the tone and speed of their voice, and only 7 percent relates to what is actually said.

Love and Chemistry

. . . .

Predictable patterns of neurochemistry emerge when we are "falling in love," and explain many of the cherished symptoms we equate with this state of being. Not surprisingly, the initial draw to become close to someone is driven by the sex hormones estrogen and testosterone in both men and women.

Love Is a Drug

. . . .

In the next stage of love, our stress response is activated, which increases our blood pressure and causes our heart to race. We experience higher levels of dopamine, the neurochemical that is responsible for creating the experience of an intense rush of pleasure. This is related to our increased energy, decreased need for sleep or food, focused attention on the other person and the relationship, and the immense satisfaction we take in the small details.

Obsessed with You

. . . .

When in newfound love, we can't stop ourselves from thinking about the other person. Italian psychologist Donatella Marazziti and her team found that the experience in your mind is related to a decrease in our

serotonin levels—to the same level that is seen in people with obsessive-compulsive disorder.

Want to Fall in Love?

. . . .

Well, New York-based psychologist Arthur Arun has found the formula. He had subjects who had never met or seen one another before reveal very intimate details about their lives for half an hour, then stare silently into one another's eyes for four minutes. A strong majority of the subjects reported feeling deeply attracted to one another after the experiment— amazingly, one couple even went on to get married.

Why not find out for yourself? You may well find that inquiries among your friends, family, and colleagues reveal confessions of intimacies exchanged early in their relationships.

5.

The Social Self

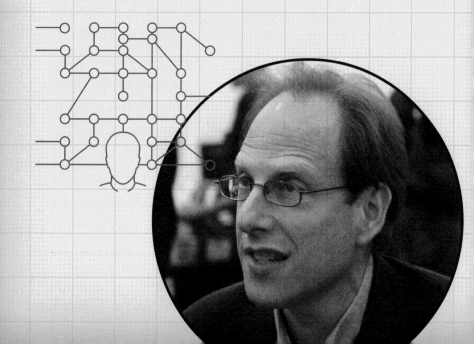

We're a profoundly social species and some of the most famous experiments in psychology have been concerned with the way we relate to each other. Why do we follow orders? Why is there so much prejudice in the world when we are all members of the same human race? We'll look at these questions as well as provide tips for improving our more personal relationships.

Prejudice

How would you sum up social history in nine words? How about: People form into groups and compete with other groups? Okay, that doesn't cover everything, but there's no question that, from families to nation-states, the tendency of people to form themselves into social groups has had a profound impact on our history. Group membership brings obvious benefits in terms of cooperation and teamwork, but an unfortunate side effect is that instead of seeing each other as individuals, we make judgments and assumptions about others based on their group membership.

Are You in My Gang or Aren't You?

Henri Tajfel and colleagues demonstrated the power of group identity in a classic study published in 1971. School children were allocated to one of two groups based purely on their preference for one of two abstract artists: Paul Klee and Wassily Kandinsky. When each child subsequently chose how to distribute money between a pair of their anonymous peers, identified only by their membership of the Klee or Kandinsky group, they showed a consistent tendency to go for the option that meant the child in their group received more money.

This instinct for group loyalty is thought to lie at the heart of much of the prejudice found in today's world. Historically, it may have been helpful for our ancestors to be able to identify fellow group members according to certain markers such as clothing or symbols (skin color would probably have varied little or not at all between neighboring tribes). The trouble is, we continue to use such shortcuts today even when they are most often meaningless. Biology shows, for example, that there is more genetic variation between members of the same racial group than there is between members of different racial groups. Unfortunately, the social cues that we use tend to be those that are most crude, such as age, gender, and race.

You're Disgusting

What's more, new research is showing that our obsession with who is or isn't in our group may be driven in part by the emotion of disgust. In the same way that instinctive disgust leads us to avoid eating old or contaminated food, the same emotion may underlie our desire to keep social outsiders, with their alien customs and beliefs, separate from our own group. Support for this idea comes from research showing that people who are more conservative also tend to be more

disgust-prone, based on their agreement with statements like: "I never let any part of my body touch the toilet seat in public restrooms."

Brain-imaging research is even showing that we are prone to viewing members of some social groups as less than human—a finding that could help explain humankind's capacity for such cruelty to others. Lasana Harris and Susan Fiske scanned the brains of university students as they looked at pictures of people from different social groups. The sight of sporting heroes, the elderly, and businessmen all triggered activity in the medial prefrontal cortex—an area of the brain associated with thinking about other people or oneself. By contrast, the sight of homeless people or drug addicts failed to provoke activity in this area, and in fact triggered a response in the areas of the brain related to disgust.

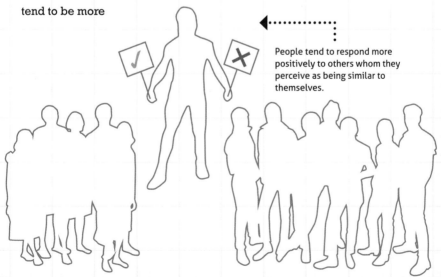

People tend to respond more positively to others whom they perceive as being similar to themselves.

Obedience to Authority

Obedience is vital to the existence of a civilized society. If the majority of people chose to disobey the rule of law, then we'd be living in anarchy. But obedience has a dark side. To some extent, it was the willingness of ordinary people to obey orders that resulted in some of history's worst atrocities.

A Shocking Experiment

One of the most famous psychology experiments of all time investigated how far people will go in their obedience to authority. In 1961 Stanley Milgram invited male participants to a Yale University lab to take part in what they were told was a study of the effects of punishment on learning. Their task was to apply electric shocks of increasing voltage to another participant (who was in reality an actor) whenever he got an answer in a verbal memory test wrong. The participants were reassured that though the shocks could be extremely painful, they would cause no permanent harm.

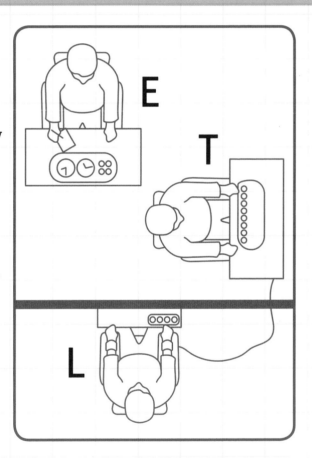

Shocks were applied by flicking a line of 30 switches, which increased in 15-volt increments up to 450 volts. The switches were also labeled in groups of four, from "Slight Shock" all the way up to "Danger: Severe Shock," with the final two groups beyond 330 volts simply marked "XXX."

The participants watched as the man playing the role of learner was strapped to a chair. The participants then returned to the adjacent room where the shock controls were housed. From the outset, the learner answered many questions incorrectly, so the participants were instructed to keep cranking up the shocks.

At 300 volts, the learner pounded the wall in protest. At 315 volts, he pounded again before ceasing to give any further answers. Beyond this point he fell completely silent.

The experimenter, a stern man in a gray lab coat, told the researchers to treat a non-response as a wrong answer and to keep increasing the voltage. There were 40 participants from a range of professions, aged between 20 and 50. How many of them do you think continued applying electric shocks right up to the highest level? Would you have continued until the end?

The answer is that 26 out of the 40 participants delivered the highest shock—two categories higher than "Danger: Severe Shock"! Milgram reported similar results in further experiments; however, it has been difficult for others to replicate his work because of ethical issues. The participants found the experiment extraordinarily stressful. Many were trembling and sweating; others had nervous laughing fits. One man had such violent convulsions that the experiment had to be aborted.

The impact of the experiment on both academic psychology and popular culture has been immense. Milgram conducted his experiments just months after the trial of Nazi war criminal Adolf Eichmann. More recently, the U.S. troops responsible for the prisoner abuse at the Abu Ghraib camp in Iraq claimed they were following orders, so the experiment and the questions it raises about obedience remain as topical as ever.

Experiments in Virtual Reality

In 2006, psychologists at University College London recreated Milgram's classic experiment in virtual reality. Participants applied shocks to a computer-animated woman whenever she made errors in a memory test. Rather than being a test of obedience, the objective of the experiment was really to see just how immersive and realistic virtual reality can be.

Remarkably, several of the participants opted to stop the experiment before delivering the strongest shock, and measures of their heart rate and sweating showed they were clearly stressed by the experience.

Issues with Group Brandstorming

Imagine you and your friends were asked to come up with as many ways as possible to increase tourism to your hometown. How would you organize yourselves? You might think your best bet would be to sit down together and have a good old brainstorming session. But in fact the research consistently shows that doing so would hamper your creativity. You'd be much better off if you each went away to think on your own, only reuniting to pool your suggestions.

In 1987 Michael Diehl and Wolfgang Stroebe listed 22 prior studies that compared the productivity of brainstorming groups with the productivity of groups in which team members worked alone before pooling their ideas. The message was clear: 18 out of 22 of the studies showed that the groups where members worked alone came up with more ideas than the brainstorming groups.

Why Is Brainstorming Still So Popular?

According to the Dutch psychologist Bernard Nijstad, when we participate in a group brainstorming session, we spend a lot of time waiting for other people to speak, which takes the pressure off us, and we also come away with a sense that plenty of ideas have been bounced around.

By contrast, when we work alone, we place a constant pressure on ourselves to come up with ideas. And if we're creatively sterile for more than a few moments, it can leave us with a sense that we are failing. It is this difference in what it feels like to work alone compared with being in a brainstorming group that Nijstad thinks underlies people's continuing faith in brainstorming.

Other ways in which brainstorming can feel more effective than working alone include memory confusion— that is, retrospectively mistaking other people's ideas for your own; and the process of "social comparison"— when we see how difficult other people are finding it to come up with ideas it can make us feel better about our own performance responsibility for actions relating to our own success and well-being.

FIVE WAYS TO BOOST GROUP CREATIVITY

- **Three is the Magic Number**
  When it comes to logic-based problem solving as opposed to idea generation, three-person groups work best. In a 2006 paper, Patrick Laughlin and colleagues tested the performance of two-, three-, four-, and five-person groups on letter-number logic problems, in which participants had to work out which letters corresponded to which numbers using as few questions as possible. The three-, four-, and five-person groups consistently outperformed the same numbers of people working alone. Crucially, however, the four- and five-person groups were no better than the three-person groups, suggesting this is the optimal number for logic-based tasks.

- **The Importance of Unity**
  Multidisciplinary teams are especially effective, but without certain dynamics in place, they can risk breaking up into cliques. Based on a study of experts working within the U.K.'s National Health Service, Doris Fay and colleagues found teams that were more multidisciplinary came up with better-quality ideas than less multidisciplinary teams only when: all team members were committed to the same cause; everyone in the team felt listened to; the team reflected on its own effectiveness; and there was plenty of contact between team members.

- **Mix up Team Membership**
  If you leave the same people in the same teams, they'll feel their groups are more friendly, but at a price. Charlan Nemeth and Margaret Ormiston showed in a 2007 study that teams with a stable membership are less creative than newly formed teams.

- **Brainstorm Alone**
  Instead, team members should work on new ideas alone before pooling their suggestions together.

- **Introduce a New Team Member**
  You might not have enough personnel to keep refreshing the entire composition of your teams as suggested elsewhere. But in a 2005 study looking at three-person teams, Hoon-Seok Choi and Leigh Thompson showed that simply swapping one team member for a newcomer boosts the creativity of a group when compared to teams with a stable composition. Crucially, newcomers didn't just bring their own ideas to

The Power of Mimics

···

We're all mimics. Have you ever noticed that when someone else yawns, you do too? You laugh, they laugh. They lean back, you lean back. Perhaps you even start using some of each other's catchphrases, or parroting one another's accents. We all perform this social dance of mimicry to varying degrees. But why do we copy each other and what effect does it have?

Imitation Really Is the Sincerest Form of Flattery

···

In a study published in 2007, William Maddux and colleagues at the INSEAD business school in Paris arranged dozens of MBA students into pairs, with one person playing the role of employer while the other acted as job candidate. Their task was to negotiate the terms of employment. Crucially, half the students were told to mimic the mannerisms of their negotiation partner.

The effects of mimicry were impressive, especially considering no formal training was involved. Students who mimicked achieved more of their own negotiation aims, and what's more, their partners benefited too, tending to come away from the discussions with more gains than the students in pairs where no one mimicked.

So what was going on? A further experiment established that student negotiators who

mimicked were rated as more trustworthy than average, suggesting that may have been the key factor. However, the effects of mimicry go way beyond the perception of the mimicker. Dutch psychologist Rick van Baaren and his colleagues invited students to their lab to rate some advertisements. While there, half the students were mimicked by one of the researchers, an experience that positively biased the way these students behaved toward everyone, not just the person

who mimicked them. For example, the mimicked students subsequently picked up more of the pens "accidentally" dropped by another of the researchers, and they also agreed to give more money to a charity than did the students who weren't mimicked.

It's almost as though there is something about being mimicked that puts us in a positive frame of mind, leading us to behave more altruistically. When what we see others doing is the same as what we're doing, it's easier for our brains to process; it's a fluent, rewarding experience. In fact, according to van Baaren, being mimicked is in some ways the default state, such that it has a negative effect on us when we're not mimicked. A study that looked at participants' brain activity showed that not being mimicked

was associated with increased activity in parts of the brain associated with negative emotions, including disgust!

Experts aren't sure why we tend to mimic each other, but from an evolutionary perspective, considering that humans have always been social animals, it certainly makes sense for us to engage in a behavior that will lead others to view us favorably. In this context, mimicry can be seen as a kind of social glue, helping build harmonious relationships. Furthermore, mimicry no doubt has advantages in terms of sheer survival value—if there is a threat to the group (for example, from a nearby wolf), it makes sense to copy what other people are doing (in this case, run and hide).

A Word of Warning

Before you try out mimicking in the real world, beware that the effects of mimicking completely backfire if people realize they are being mimicked. Mimicking is something that occurs naturally between interacting partners—if you deliberately try to imitate the body language of another person you may risk their noticing.

A possible way to reduce the likelihood of this happening is to introduce a delay before you copy another person's actions. So if they cross their legs, wait a few seconds before crossing your own.

When someone **mimics** our actions it boosts feelings of positivity and makes us feel more comfortable around them.

Culture and Perspective-Taking

The culture we're brought up in shapes the way we think about ourselves and others, even to the point of affecting the response of our brains to simple visual tasks. Most research in this area has focused on differences in perspective-taking between people raised in so-called collectivist cultures, such as China, Japan, and Korea, and those raised in more individualistic cultures, such as in North America and Western Europe.

Put crudely, in collectivist cultures people are encouraged to harmonize and adjust to others and to act appropriately. By contrast, people in individualistic cultures are encouraged to know what they want and to go out and get it.

These cultural differences can affect the extent to which individuals adopt the perspective of other people. When children reach the age of about four, they develop the ability to see things from other people's point of view. The effect of an individualistic culture is not to remove this ability, but rather to affect people's tendency to use it.

In a 2007 study by Shali Wu and Boaz Keysar at the University of Chicago, 20 non-Asian Americans and 20 Chinese people played a game that involved a researcher directing them to move objects in a shelflike grid that could be viewed from both sides. Crucially, views of some of the boxes in the grid were blocked off from the researcher's side only, a fact that was apparent to the participants.

Boxing Clever

Wu and Keysar timed how long it took the participants to respond to simple instructions, such as "Move the block up two squares," which were ambiguous only if the participants failed to take into account the researcher's perspective. For instance, there might have been two blocks, but only one visible to the researcher. Wu and Keysar found that the American participants were slower to respond than the Chinese, for example asking, "Which block do you mean?"—thus revealing their failure to take account of the researcher's perspective.

Thinking of Others

In another study published the same year, Angela Leung at Singapore

Management University and Dov Cohen at the University of Illinois at Urbana-Champaign showed strikingly that when European Americans think about themselves they do so from a first-person perspective, whereas Asian Americans view themselves from a third-person perspective.

In one experiment, participants were told stories, their interpretation of which affected their understanding of subsequent ambiguous instructions. For example, one story involved a scenario in which the participant had gone to meet a friend at a skyscraper, but as they traveled in the elevator up to the 94th floor, their friend was in another elevator heading down to reception. Next, the same participants were given a map showing the city "Jackson" and asked to mark the location of the city "Jamestown" on it, which they were told, ambiguously, was the next city "after" Jackson on the north–south highway. Leung and Cohen found the Asian Americans were more likely to mark Jamestown as the next city south of Jackson, whereas the European Americans were more likely to mark it as the next city north. This corresponds with the idea that the Asian Americans had visualized the skyscraper story from their friend's perspective (their friend going down in the elevator biasing them to place Jamestown south), whereas the European Americans had visualized the story from their own perspective (their journey up the elevator biasing them to place Jamestown north).

Our **culture** can influence whether we view things from our own perspective or that of others.

Personal Relationships

We're social animals and close relationships are essential to our mental well-being. There's even research showing that married people live longer than singles. Robert Kaplan and Richard Kronick at the University of California checked on the marital status of tens of thousands of people in 1989 and then looked to see who was still alive in 1997. Compared with married people, singles were far more likely to have died during that time, especially if they had never been married.

Meanwhile, research by Constantine Sedikides at Southampton University in the U. K. has shown that merely thinking about people who are close to us can have protective effects on our mental well-being. Participants whom Sedikides asked to think about an intimate other were subsequently more receptive to being told by researchers about weaknesses in their own mental abilities, presumably because thinking about a loved one had acted as a shield for their self-esteem. Here are four tips for a healthy relationship:

1. Be Generous with Your Support

Providing ample, unconditional support to your partner won't make them needy, rather it will lead them toward greater independence and self-sufficiency—a finding psychologist Brooke Feeney of Carnegie Mellon University has dubbed the "dependency paradox."

One study of 165 married couples found that husbands and wives who received plenty of unconditional support from their partners were more likely to have achieved a stated goal six months later, and to report being self-sufficient and feeling secure.

2. Keep in Touch

There are times in life when it can be difficult to maintain our closest friendships. Psychologists Debra Oswald and Eddie Clark studied 137 students who were making their transition from high school to college.

By the following spring, only 55 percent of them still considered their best friend from high school to be their closest friend. Which friendships survived? Oswald and Clark found that geographical distance was irrelevant. Friendship survival depended on frequent phone contact, the sharing of private thoughts, and being cheerful and upbeat when together. What's more, the students who remained close to their best friend from high school were less likely to complain of loneliness during their first year at college.

3. Write About Your Relationship

Writing about your relationship could increase its longevity, according to a study by Richard Slatcher and James Pennebaker at the University of Texas at Austin. Of 86 heterosexual undergrads, Slatcher and Pennebaker asked half to write about their romantic relationship for 20 minutes a day for three days. The other half wrote about their daily activities. Three months later, 77 percent of the students who had written about their relationship were still with the same partner, compared with just 52 percent of the students who had written about their activities. Analysis of instant messaging communication between couples showed that writing about their relationship led them to use more positive emotional words when communicating with each other.

Relationships in which couples feel they share things equally are likely to last longer.

4. Keep Things Equal

According to social exchange theory, if one partner in a relationship perceives that they are receiving less than they are giving, in terms of a range of factors including love, money, status, and sex, then prospects for the future of the relationship won't be good. Susan Sprecher at Illinois State University followed the progress of 101 student couples for nearly five years. She found that participants who felt they gave more than they received tended to report feeling less satisfied and less committed to their relationship, and there was a greater likelihood of the relationship ending. However, in some cases it may be that a lack of relationship satisfaction and commitment leads people to feel that they are receiving less from a relationship than they are giving.

Writing about your relationship may boost your feelings toward your partner.

Antonio Damasio

Antonio Damasio is an influential neurologist and neuroscientist, perhaps best known for his popular books about the biological basis of consciousness and emotions. These include *The Feeling of What Happens* and *Descartes' Error*, both translated into more than 30 languages.

Damasio hopes that work on the biological bases of emotions and decision-making can help to reach a solution to human conflict, and to solve the mystery of consciousness.

Moral Decision-Making

Damasio has also shown the role played by emotions in our moral decision-making. Consider the dilemma of whether or not you as a hostage would be prepared to kill another hostage in return for the release of yourself and eight children. What would you do? Most people recoil from the prospect of deliberately killing another, so choose instead to sacrifice the freedom of the majority for the life of that person. By contrast, patients with damage to the ventromedial prefrontal cortex (who lack emotions) make more pragmatic choices in these kinds of situations— favoring killing one person for the benefit of the majority. However, when it comes to less personal moral choices, these patients make the same choices as healthy people.

Damasio was born in Lisbon, Portugal, and studied medicine at the University of Lisbon. Today, he is David Dornsife Professor of Neuroscience and Director of the Brain and Creativity Institute at the University of Southern California. He has earned countless prizes and is a member of the Institute of Medicine of the National Academy of Sciences.

Damasio and his wife Hanna (also a respected neuroscientist) study brain-damaged patients, and use brain-imaging techniques in an attempt to understand the neurological basis of the self, the emotions, and decision-making.

TEST OUT THE SOMATIC-MARKER HYPOTHESIS

Experts used to think of decision-making as being a purely rational process, but one of Antonio Damasio's best-known theories is the somatic-marker hypothesis, which outlines the key role played by emotions in decision-making.

One way Damasio has tested his somatic-marker hypothesis is by using a gambling task designed to capture the rewards, punishments, and uncertainty of life. To try this out on your friends, create 100 cards and arrange them into four piles. Cards in piles A and B carry rewards of $100 each, but one in every ten cards has a penalty of $1,250. Cards in piles C and D have rewards of just $50, with one $250 penalty card in every ten. Arrange the card piles appropriately, without giving away any details. Then, ask a friend to take one card at a time from any of the piles, with the aim to accumulate as much money as possible in 50 cards. Watch how they play and keep a score of their earnings for comparison.

At first, your friend won't know what to expect and will probably be drawn to the piles that carry the higher rewards. But as they play on, they should instinctively start to take more cards from piles C and D—the best strategy for earning more money. Damasio showed that emotions play a key role in successful performance at this task. Patients with damage to the ventromedial prefrontal cortex, who have normal intelligence but impaired emotions, continue taking from piles A and B—a behavior that reflects their abysmal decision-making in real life. Problem gamblers also show this pattern.

Damasio also measured the emotional response (based on the sweatiness of their fingers) of healthy people as they played. Even before they'd begun to take cards consistently from piles C and D, Damasio found these participants showed an emotional response before picking up cards from the disadvantageous piles. This suggests it is our emotional response to the cards that guides our decision-making, even before we fully realize it.

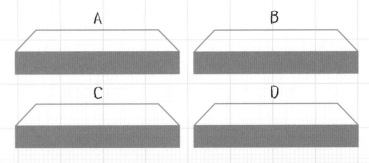

Mindblindness

Central to successful socializing is our ability to represent to ourselves the perspective of other people—to imagine ourselves in their shoes. Psychologists call this having a "Theory of Mind" because, literally, it is about forming theories of other people's mental states. However, in children and adults with autism or Asperger's Syndrome, this ability can be severely impaired, leading to what some experts have dubbed "Mindblindness."

Simon
Baron-Cohen

There are several ways this manifests as the child with autism grows up. For example, a typical 14-month-old toddler will follow another person's gaze to see what they are looking at, whereas the child with autism or Asperger's will usually do this far less. A typical nine-year-old will understand when a social faux pas has occurred—those instances when someone has done something embarrassing or that might upset or offend others. By contrast, children of that age, and even adults, who have autism or Asperger's, find it difficult to recognize these kinds of social transgressions.

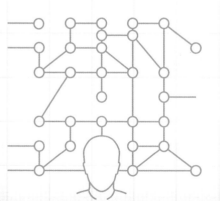

People with autism tend to be very good at understanding and analyzing systems, such as sentence structure, weather patterns, or calendars. The autism expert Simon Baron-Cohen has developed a theory that is based on understanding this mixture of poor empathizing with superior systematizing. His approach recognizes that we all vary on these dimensions, and that autism merely represents an extreme end of a normal continuum.

Autistic Pride

You may have heard of autistic savants—people with autism who, alongside their difficulties, have a rare, extreme talent, such as for drawing in intricate detail, or for calculating instantly what day a given date falls on. However, a growing movement is recognizing the potential abilities of all people with autism and Asperger's, not just the savants. This perspective argues that the autistic brain doesn't have anything wrong with it, it's just different. Advocates say we should celebrate the "neuro-diversity" between individuals rather than seek a "cure" for autism.

ARE YOU AN EMPATHIZER OR SYSTEMATIZER?

1. I prefer to speak to people in person rather than emailing.
TRUE/FALSE

2. When I listen to music, I enjoy recognizing the way it is structured.
TRUE/FALSE

3. I find it hard to predict how people will feel in a given situation.
TRUE/FALSE

4. If I were buying a cellphone, I wouldn't be interested in the details of how it works.   TRUE/FALSE

5. If someone starts to get upset, it can make me get upset too.
TRUE/FALSE

6. I have my clothes organized carefully according to type.   TRUE/FALSE

7. I don't like to think of animals suffering.
TRUE/FALSE

8. I'm not keen on fixed routines or plans.
TRUE/FALSE

9. I've been told before that I am sometimes insensitive, but I can't see why.
TRUE/FALSE

10. Bus and train timetables are easy to understand.   TRUE/FALSE

11. I can usually tell how other people are feeling.   TRUE/FALSE

12. I'm not bothered with the "small print."
TRUE/FALSE

Empathizing: Score a point each time you answer true to items 1, 5, 7, 11, and each time you answer false to 3 or 9. The more points you scored, the more of an empathizer you are.

Systematizing: Score a point each time you answer true to items 2, 6, 10 and each time you answer false to 4, 8, and 12. The more points you score, the more of a systematizer you are.

People with autism and Asperger's tend to score very high on systematizing and very low on empathizing. There are also sex differences: men tend to score higher on the systematizing scale but lower on the empathizing scale relative to women. This is consistent with the far higher prevalence of autism (4:1) and Asperger's (9:1) among men relative to women, which has led Baron-Cohen to propose that autism represents an extreme form of the male brain.

Personality

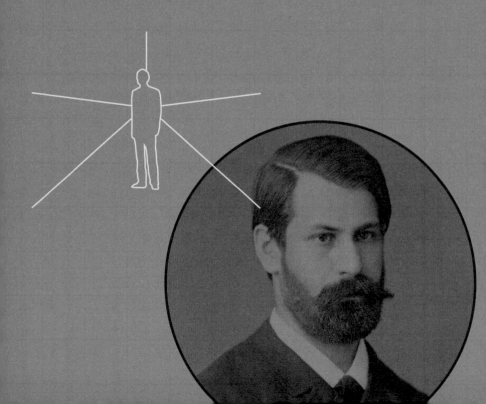

For over a hundred years psychologists have been fascinated with how best to categorize and describe the different types of personality based on their enduring behavioral and emotional characteristics. We'll look at the tests they use and the emerging consensus on the different types of personality traits. Also: why do some people make great leaders, and what happens when personality goes awry?

Projective Tests

Personality is one of those concepts that we're always referring to in everyday conversation, yet which we seldom stop to consider in any depth. On the one hand, we're all unique, so what's the point of saying anything about Average Joe's personality beyond the fact that his character is like, well, Average Joe?

On the other hand, there are certain situations—imagine having been starving and then finally getting something to eat—in which we'd presumably all respond in pretty much the same way, with sighs of relief and grunts of satisfaction. From this perspective, Joe Bloggs's personality, like the rest of us, is simply human. Usually, therefore, when we talk about someone's personality, we're navigating between these extremes: we're saying something interesting about the enduring ways in which this person is similar to some people, and yet different from others. More on this in the Big Five Personality Factors (pp. 100–101).

Measuring Personality

A problem with measuring people's personality is that if you ask someone about themselves, they're likely to tell you what they think you want to hear: "Yes, I'm a caring person," "No, I never get jealous." It's to overcome these "issues of social desirability," as they're known, that some psychologists advocate

the use of projective tests such as the famous Rorschach inkblot test and the Thematic Apperception Test (TAT). The idea with these open-ended tests is that we can't help but project something of who we are in the way that we interpret ambiguous pictures.

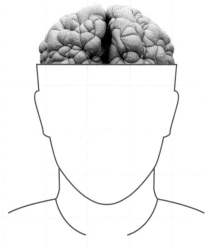

It must be stated that these projective tests are controversial. The whole point of psychology is that it applies the objective scrutiny of science to human nature. For this reason, contemporary psychology dictates that effective tests must be both reliable and valid. Reliability refers

Psychologists use the **Rorschach inkblot** to analyze personality traits and emotional well-being.

to how similar scores on the test will be with repeated testing by the same individual, or with repeated scoring by different markers. Individuals who are matched on whatever is being measured should also score similarly. Validity refers to whether the test measures what it claims to be measuring.

Critics of the Rorschach test and TAT claim that they are lacking on both these criteria. The same participant, they say, is likely to respond in wildly different ways on repeated testing, and two different judges are likely to score their answers in different ways. And arguably, it's not always clear what the tests are actually measuring, so in that sense they lack validity. Having said all that, many psychologists, especially in the United States, do still endorse these tests.

The Rorschach Test
....

Devised by the Swiss psychiatrist Hermann Rorschach, the inkblot test involves the

participant looking at ten symmetrical inkblots and describing what they see. Participants' responses to each blot are traditionally scored according to three factors: the parts of the inkblot that they focus on; the shape, form, color, and perceived movement that they describe; and the content that they interpret the blot as showing, especially in terms of the presence of human, animal, or anatomical shapes. The image above shows one of the original blots used by Rorschach. What do you see?

The Thematic Apperception Test
....

Devised by the Harvard psychologist Henry Murray in the 1930s, this test involves the participant looking at a series of deliberately ambiguous line drawings showing one or more people in various situations. The participants' task is to tell the story of what is happening before, during, and after the scene. The psychologist will make inferences about the participant based on these stories.

The Big Five Personality Factors

As discussed in the preceding pages, personality is about describing those enduring ways in which a person is similar to some people yet different from others. If you consider the number of words we have for describing each other—lively, shy, considerate, reckless, humble, proud, arrogant, brave... the list goes on and on—then you'll soon realize what a daunting task it has been for psychology to find a scientific way to capture the essence of what someone is like.

Typical **neurotic personality traits** include anxiety, fear, envy, and loneliness.

The science of personality isn't just about description, it's also about prediction—someone's personality can impact on a range of outcomes, anything from the likely success of their marriage to their probable longevity.

The Key Factors of You

Various philosophers and psychologists have proposed the key factors that they think capture personality. For example, Hans Eysenck argued for the existence of two personality dimensions: extraversion vs. introversion and neuroticism vs. stability. A third dimension, psychoticism vs. socialization, was added to his theory later. Raymond Cattell meanwhile proposed that there are 16 factors underlying personality: warmth, reasoning, emotional stability, dominance, to name just a few.

After years of research and with the help of a statistical technique called factor analysis, most psychologists now agree there are five main traits underlying personality, known as the Big Five Factors. These were arrived at by stripping out all the redundant ways of describing people. For example, take the following personality traits: creative, imaginative, eccentric. Research shows that if a person scores high on one of these traits, then they're likely to score high on the other two. In other words, these three traits are really all describing the more fundamental attribute that psychologists call "Openness." The other four Big Factors are: Extraversion (how outgoing vs. quiet a person is), Neuroticism (how prone to worry vs. stable), Conscientiousness (how diligent vs. reckless), and Agreeableness (how trusting vs. hostile).

knocked into a given state, such as anxiety or arousal, depending on the situation.

How Stable Is Personality?

Psychologists disagree about this. The notion that personality is fixed, come what may, has been dubbed the "fundamental attribution error" by critics who believe situations play a powerful role in the way that we behave. Both extremes of the argument can be empowering or disheartening depending on how you interpret them.

The idea that personality is fixed is reassuring in the sense that it suggests we will stay true to ourselves, no matter what life throws

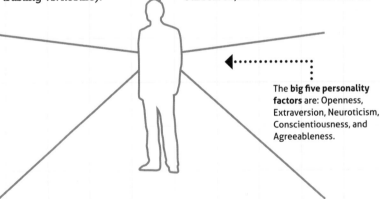

The **big five personality factors** are: Openness, Extraversion, Neuroticism, Conscientiousness, and Agreeableness.

A mixture of genetics and early life experiences determine our scores on the five factors. Daniel Nettle at the University of Newcastle in th UK has said that the Big Five Factors can be viewed as shorthand for the way that a person is wired up. He says the factors are akin to a series of thermostats, with people differing in the thresholds at which they are

at us. On the other hand, we might not like ourselves much, and this fixed view of personality implies that we're stuck the way we are without any capacity for change. So to people who dream of change, the strong situationist approach to personality is appealing, arguing as it does that we can all become whoever we want to be, given the right circumstances.

Leadership Material

History is littered with both inspiring (Winston Churchill, Joan of Arc) and notorious (Adolf Hitler, Pol Pot) leaders, and so perhaps it is no surprise that early psychological theories about leadership dwelt on the kind of person who makes an influential leader. However, this "great man" approach has since fallen out of favor as psychologists have recognized that what makes a good leader varies with the situation and with the group that is being led.

According to the psychologists Stephen Reicher, Alexander Haslam, and Michael Platow, effective leaders are people who are seen to represent the interests of their followers. Members of a coherent group will have a shared identity with shared goals, and their leader, if effective, will be seen as representing them and working toward their goals.

Many view **Winston Churchill (1874–1965)** as one of Britain's greatest-ever leaders. As prime minister during World War II, he led the country in the fight against Nazism.

Taking this perspective on leadership generates predictions that the latest research appears to support.

For example, one experiment showed that the efforts of team members diminished as their leader's pay increased by up to triple of what they earned. That is presumably because followers struggle to identify with a leader who, they perceive, is not equal to them. Some of history's recent leaders have heeded this lesson. Just think of George W. Bush in his cowboy hat and jeans, or Gandhi in his villager's dress—these leaders were saying to their followers: "I am just like you."

Mahatma Gandhi (1869–1948) wore simple clothes made of locally grown and spun cotton.

FOUR SURPRISING FINDINGS ABOUT LEADERSHI

1. Appearances seem to matter. Nicholas Rule and Nalini Ambady asked 100 students to rate the appearance of 50 faces. Unbeknown to the students, these were the faces of chief execs of America's most and least profitable largest companies. The leaders of the most profitable companies were rated as more competent, dominant, and mature than those of the least profitable companies. It's not clear whether working for a certain type of company influences the appearance of its chief exec; whether having a chief exec with a certain kind of face affects the fortunes of that company; or whether successful vs. unsuccessful companies differ in the kind of looks they go for in their chief executives.

2. A strong leader isn't always a good thing. An investigation of several Chinese companies found that in those organizations with a good customer service ethos, strong team leaders had a negligible effect on external customer service. According to Harry Hui and colleagues it's possible the strong leaders were out of sync with their organization's broader service climate.

standardized ways of dealing with customers, while the strong leader may preach innovation.

3. Effective leadership is sometimes associated with a hesitant speaking style. Fifty-four participants rated the leadership potential of a fictitious man called Richard, based on one of two versions of a telephone conversation. In one version he seemed assertive and confident; in the other he spoke with doubt and hesitation. Those participants who were told that Richard was being considered for a company that valued employees' ability to work alone rated him as a more suitable leader if they'd heard his confident conversation style. By contrast, the participants told the company favored cooperation among staff rated Richard as a better potential leader if they'd heard his hesitant conversation.

4. It helps to be the first born. Studies have found that first-born children are over-represented among leaders of countries around the world. A study in 2003 by Rudy Andeweg and Steef Van Den Berg found that only children are

Perfectionist Personalities

Do you often experience the nagging feeling that you could have done better? Do you find that you are always criticizing yourself? If so, it sounds like you may well have a perfectionist personality.

Being a perfectionist is a double-edged sword—in moderation it is associated with high attainment, but taken to extremes it can lead to mental-health problems. People with an extremely perfectionist personality are at increased risk of developing anxiety disorders, eating disorders, and even committing suicide.

Whether perfectionism leads to problems usually depends on other aspects of a person's personality. For example, setting high standards for oneself can be a good thing, and many high achievers of course do just that, but if someone can't cope with not reaching those high standards then that's when problems can occur.

A study carried out by British psychologists Rory O'Connor and Daryl O'Connor, meanwhile, found that perfectionist students were at increased risk of psychological distress only if they also tended to deal with problems by avoiding them. Neither avoidant coping nor perfectionism were problematic on their own.

What Is Obsessive-Compulsive Disorder?

Excessive perfectionism is strongly associated with obsessive-compulsive disorder (OCD). People with OCD experience nagging obsessive thoughts, such as about cleanliness or safety, which they are only able to relieve by performing certain compulsions. These compulsions normally take the form of repeated washing or checking. The condition becomes problematic when it starts interfering with everyday life.

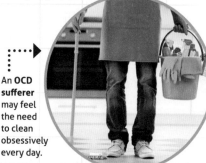

An **OCD sufferer** may feel the need to clean obsessively every day.

ARE YOU A MAXIMIZER OR A SATISFICER?

According to Barry Schwartz at Swarthmore College, one kind of perfectionist who is particularly prone to problems is the "maximizer." Maximizers are characterized by their determination always to make the best choice—which is an impossible task. There's always one more shop to look in, one more restaurant to try. Satisficers, on the other hand, are better equipped to deal with the explosion of choices available in the modern world. The satisficer is happy to settle for what is good enough, without feeling pressure to seek out the very best.

The following test is inspired by Schwartz's own maximization scale. For each of the following eight statements, score from 1 (completely disagree) to 7 (completely agree).

1. I'm always imagining what a different kind of life from my own could be like.

2. I can't stand those lists you get in magazines and on TV shows in which they count down the best of this or the best of that.

3. I spend ages shopping because I like to compare the same product between stores.

4. I rarely look at job ads—I'm content with the job I've got.

5. When I'm confronted with a choice, I like to consider all the options available to me, even those that aren't on the table.

6. I'm quick at writing emails and cellphone texts because I rarely worry about how I've phrased things.

7. When I'm watching a TV show, I often find myself wondering if I'm missing something better on another channel.

8. When I met my partner I knew he/she was the one for me, or I don't expect to work through loads of relationships before finding my perfect match.

• •

SCORING

Subtract your points for items 2, 4, 6, and 8 from your points for items 1, 3, 5, and 7. If you're left with a positive score, then you're more of a maximizer than a satisficer, whereas if you're left with a negative score, you're more of a satisficer. According to Schwartz, maximizers should beware—the combination of their mentality with the abundance of choice in the modern world could lead to frustration and unhappiness.

Multiple Personalities

We've all heard of Dr. Jekyll and Mr. Hyde, but can people really have more than one personality? It's incredibly rare, but yes, there are indeed reports of people having multiple alter egos—a condition that was known as multiple personality disorder, but which today is referred to as dissociative identity disorder (DID).

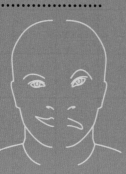

Perhaps the best-known case is that of Sybil, who in the 1970s was reported to possess 16 different personalities. Her story was first told in a book by journalist Flora Schreiber and has since been made into a mini-series and a film. Another case made famous in the 1950s was Eve, who eventually claimed 22 different alter egos.

The diagnosis of DID is extremely controversial, not least because it is difficult to ascertain how much a person with the condition is acting or responding to suggestion. It doesn't help that alter egos have often been identified under hypnosis. Also, the number of reported cases tends to rise and fall dramatically depending on the profile of the condition—an "epidemic" occurred in the 1980s and 1990s when the condition reached its highest profile.

Diagnosing Multiple Personalities

Today DID is recognized as one of a cluster of psychiatric conditions, alongside depersonalization disorder (feeling that you are no longer real), dissociative fugue (forgetting who you are and your life story), and dissociative amnesia

Multiple personalities may develop in childhood as a way of blocking out traumatic memories.

(forgetting certain past experiences in your life). A diagnosis of these conditions is made only in the absence of a clear organic cause, such as brain injury or disease. The preference of contemporary psychiatry has been to shift the emphasis away from the idea of multiple personalities, to focus more on the apparent breakdown in consciousness and memory seen in patients, hence the association of DID with fugue states (see panel) and depersonalization.

A popular theory is that multiple personalities and other forms of dissociation emerge as a way of coping with extreme and continuous trauma, especially in childhood. This would appear to make some intuitive sense. For example, in some patients only one or some of their personalities will have access to memories of the trauma they claim to have experienced in childhood, while the other personalities will appear to be protected from the pain of these recalled experiences. However, these observations are based almost entirely on the self-report of patients and there are clear problems with suggestibility in therapy.

On balance it seems that, in very rare circumstances, some form of personality splitting probably can occur and is probably related in some way to experiencing trauma. To date there has been very little experimental study of people with apparent multiple personalities— for example, to see how the different personalities score on established personality tests.

THOUGHT EXPERIMENT: LEGAL ISSUES

The dissociative disorders raise all sorts of difficulties when it comes to judging criminal responsibility. For example, imagine a suspect in court has been diagnosed by a psychiatrist as having DID, with multiple personalities. What if the suspect claims that their dominant, host personality did not commit the crime; that the offender was one of their other personalities? Should the entire person be held accountable? Or consider the case of fugue states, in which the person has forgotten who they are. Should convicted criminals be held just as culpable even if they have no recollection of the crimes they committed? Not only can these be awkward issues, but of course such scenarios also raise the suspicion of malingering (pretending to be ill). This happened in the real-life case of the "Hillside Strangler" Kenneth Bianchi, who, with his cousin, was charged with several murders in 1970s Los Angeles. Bianchi claimed to have multiple personality disorder and that one of his alter egos had committed the murders, but court psychologists decided he was malingering, and he was sentenced to life imprisonment.

Disordered Personalities

People diagnosed with a personality disorder have extreme character traits that cause them to find life difficult, so that they, and often those close to them, suffer as a result.

There are ten forms of personality disorder listed in the current version of psychiatry's diagnostic bible, *The Diagnostic and Statistical Manual, IV*. These are: schizoid, schizotypal, paranoid (known collectively as the odd/eccentric cluster); antisocial, borderline, histrionic, narcissistic (the dramatic/erratic cluster); and avoidant, dependent, and obsessive-compulsive (the anxious/avoidant cluster).

The whole notion of personality disorders has proven to be extremely controversial. Critics have asked how it can make any sense to label someone with a personality disorder if experts can't even agree on what exactly personality is or how to measure it. And anyway, these critics add, isn't there a large amount of subjectivity involved?

Indeed, you can imagine that a Hollywood actor teleported to an English village might be judged by locals to be narcissistic. Likewise, a dedicated Wall Street trader might, if transported to an Amsterdam café, be perceived as worryingly obsessive. The scientific soundness of the personality disorder concept is further undermined by the fact that the same person will often meet the diagnostic criteria for several different types of personality disorder.

Nonetheless, despite these concerns, the consensus among the mental-health professions is that personality disorders do exist. There can be little doubt that there are people in the world who struggle persistently with life, at least in part because of their pervasive personality traits. For these individuals, identifying that they have a personality disorder can be a crucial first step on the path to helping them.

How Common Is It?

According to a recent report published by the British Psychological Society, around 10 percent of the population have a personality disorder. Perhaps unsurprisingly, rates of personality disorder are far higher among psychiatric inpatients and outpatients, and are most prevalent of all among prison inmates, where some studies have reported rates as high as 70 percent.

Many **prisoners** are people who suffer from personality disorders.

What's the Cause?

Some aspects of our personality are doubtless inherited, but we're also shaped by our upbringing and by our ongoing circumstances and experiences. Research shows that physical and sexual abuse in childhood can predispose people toward developing a personality disorder, as can parental alcoholism and parents' failure to supervise or discipline their children.

What Is Someone with a Personality Disorder Like?

It's all very well reading about the notion of a personality disorder, but what is someone with this diagnosis really like? Hopefully these fictional examples will help explain.

Sally (avoidant personality) was a successful academic despite her life-long shyness and introversion. However, she left her research position because she did not feel comfortable in meetings and hated delivering presentations. She started staying in on Fridays, instead of going to the pub. After initially claiming she was fine, Sally admitted to her physician that her shyness had become debilitating. She was referred to a specialist mental-health team for further assessment and help.

Christopher (antisocial personality) was first charged with a criminal offence at the age of 13 after stealing a car. He spent his teens in and out of care, committing acts of vandalism and theft. As a young adult, he was jailed for a serious violent assault. He shows no remorse.

As well as demonstrating the kinds of people who are likely to be diagnosed with a personality disorder, these examples also show why the concept can be contentious. Does Sally really have a personality disorder that needs treating, or is she just very shy? Does Christopher have a personality disorder or is he just a nasty, mean person?

A child subjected to violence, sexual abuse, or parental neglect may be more susceptible to developing a **personality disorder** in adult life.

Sigmund Freud

Sigmund Freud, the grandfather of psychoanalysis, started out as a hard-nosed scientist and medic. After qualifying in medicine from the University of Vienna, Austria, in 1881, he went on to study the reproductive organs of the eel.

Today his influence is felt beyond psychology; in literature, painting, and anthropology. Freud ended his days in London, having fled the Nazi occupation of Austria.

Echoes of Freud in Modern Neuroscience

Freud's work is often dismissed as a form of "pre-science," relying as it did on his detailed investigations of single case studies, rather than on the repeated, controlled testing of participant groups. Moreover, Freud's proposal that the mind is made up of an id, ego, and superego is viewed by many as seriously outdated. By contrast, other experts recognize that Freud would have been the first to seek a biological basis for his theories, had he had access to modern techniques.

Freud also published early works on aphasia (loss of language due to brain injury). However, it wasn't until he studied under the celebrated neurologist Jean-Martin Charcot at the famous Salpêtrière Hospital in Paris, that Freud's metamorphosis into a psychologist and therapist really took off.

In Paris, Freud met patients diagnosed with hysteria. From this moment Freud set out to develop a comprehensive theory of the mind. Groundbreaking studies followed, including *The Interpretation of Dreams* and *Beyond the Pleasure Principle*. Thanks to Freud, the psychoanalytic movement was born.

Anosognosia

Freud suggested that we have defense mechanisms that protect us from unacceptable or unbearable truths. Modern-day neurologists have identified a condition, observed among some neurological patients, known as anosognosia, which strongly resembles these kinds of defense mechanisms. Patients with anosognosia, who have damage to the right parietal region of their brains, appear to be in complete denial about their disabilities. For example, a woman with a paralyzed arm will refuse to accept there is anything wrong with it, and will even concoct elaborate excuses for why she isn't using her afflicted limb.

Dreams as Wish Fulfillment

Freud said that when we're asleep, the base desires of the id are given more freedom as the ego and superego are at rest. This situation manifests as dreams, which can represent our true wishes in all their unashamed glory. Early neuroscience findings debunked this idea as they suggested dreams are associated with the stage of sleep known as Rapid Eye Movement (REM) sleep, which is itself triggered by processes in the brain stem, not by brain areas involved with motivation. More recent findings, however, have shown that dreaming is not confined to REM sleep and that frontal parts of the brain involved in motivation do indeed play a part in the production of our nocturnal adventures.

Hidden Motives

Freud proposed that much of our mental life is beyond conscious awareness; that our motives are driven by subconscious desires. Consistently with this, modern social psychology has demonstrated a raft of astonishing ways in which we're influenced by factors of which we're unaware.

Repression

Freud said that as part of our defense mechanisms, our mind actively represses unpleasant memories. Modern-day researchers have shown that intentional forgetting is indeed possible and does affect the likelihood of memories being recalled in the future. Michael Anderson and colleagues presented participants with unrelated word pairs (for example, ordeal/roach). Later they were presented with the first word from each pair, and asked either to recall its partner or not to think about its partner. Not only was the latter condition associated with a unique pattern of brain activity, repressed words were also harder to recall when tested later on.

When we sleep, the desires of the id come to the fore and our true wishes are manifested as dreams.

7

Stress and Anxiety

Adrenaline-fueled fear and panic can save our lives when we experience them at the right times. For some people, however, these processes are triggered inappropriately, as part of irrational phobias or panic disorder. This chapter covers these conditions. Even when a stress-response is appropriate, a life-threatening traumatic event can leave a person with terrible psychological scars. We'll also look at this phenomenon, known as post-traumatic stress disorder.

Handling Change

Many of the most natural human experiences involve change. In fact change is indivisible from the passage of time. So why can it be so difficult to handle? Speaking in general terms, one of the biggest causes of stress and anxiety is having to adapt to change.

Researchers know that routine experiences get encoded in our brains in specific ways. It has even been shown that things as simple as taking a different route to work, trying to write with the opposite hand to usual, or just being in a room after rearranging the furniture give the brain a healthy, stimulating jolt.

The reality seems to be that we become programmed to our routines, creating an attachment even to things that would otherwise seem quite insignificant. We may have been sad to see the old gas station on the corner torn down, even if we considered it an eyesore. We develop attachments to the things we are used to seeing, doing, and knowing.

Even when change is "for the better," there tends to be a reaction of anxiety toward it. Almost by definition change necessarily means the unknown. Especially as we age, the unknown seems to inspire fear or discomfort to a greater extent.

Adapting to Change

The tendency to seek peace externally instead of internally can also contribute to making change more difficult to adapt to. If we are unhappy, we may look to our lives to see "what is to blame." We may make an external change without examining our internal lives to see what we ourselves may have been contributing to the situation. If this is the case, then we can easily find the same complaints or habits emerging in the new environment, creating further disappointment and distress.

Several other mechanisms in our thought process can further contribute to making change difficult to adapt to. These include the fact that our thoughts filter our experiences, to such a degree that our perceptions slant toward what

As we get **older**, dealing with change and learning new skills can be daunting.

can be a distorted reality. What is in actuality a minor degree of difference can be perceived as a "world of difference." This makes it much more difficult to adapt to change, because what is truly only a little different is seen as a huge change.

HOW DO YOU FEEL ABOUT CHANGE?

Which of the following describes you the best?

(a) I tend to get bored in places after doing the same things for too long. I enjoy starting new jobs or new career paths. I am continually seeking new thrills and trying new things, new foods, and new hobbies. I thrive on new experiences and am always making new friends. I love living in different cultures and consider myself a "travel junkie."

(b) I have lived in the same place for a long time and cherish my deep roots and sense of community. I like to know what to expect, and I am more comfortable with routine and stability. I tend to keep the same job for long periods of time, and the friends I see most often are the friends I have had for a long time.

ANSWERS

People who fall in the first category are those who "enjoy change," and may feel stifled if they do not experience it; however, this can still be viewed as staying within their comfort zone and, for them, to change things often can in itself still become a routine.

People who thrive on change are often at their happiest when visiting new places.

Anxiety

....

An experienced rock climber was undertaking a difficult climb when he felt the rocks that he was clinging to suddenly give way. He fell backward toward the ground, with a big chunk of rock falling closely after him. Sure to be crushed under its weight, he hit the ground. The rock fell on him, but incredibly, by summoning almost supernatural strength, he was able to "catch" and repel the rock away from him. He was hurt, but survived.

Fight or Flight

....

Our "fight or flight" mechanism is driven by the neuro-chemical hormone adrenaline. When something in our environment is strong enough to trigger the response, it results in a range of psycho-physiological responses to the impending danger. The responses include increased pupil size, so that more information can enter the eye, increased heart rate, so that oxygen can be pumped to the muscles and brain, and greater conversion of glycogen to glucose, so that rapidly contracting muscles and essential organs are supplied with increased energy.

The natural essence of anxiety enables us to remove ourselves from or prepare to combat potentially dangerous situations. While we rarely interpret stress or anxiety as healthy or welcome, the reality is that both are very natural and often useful guides for decision-making processes.

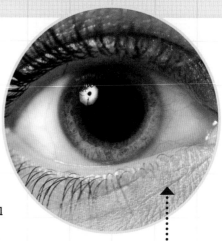

When under threat, adrenaline pumps into the bloodstream, causing the pupils to dilate.

As a society we have a tendency to qualify emotions and experiences as "good" or "bad," and to rapidly seek to get out of any emotional state that we do not regard as pleasurable. When we don't feel "well," we continually focus on how to "feel better," and this often means a struggle to fight or drown out our feelings. In reality there are no "bad" emotions. Anxiety, and other emotions that are unpleasant to feel, such as anger, are all natural parts of the human experience. They are all important, and equally valid. It is what we choose to do with these emotions, however, rather than the emotions themselves, which can clearly be good or bad.

Dealing with Stress

Continued stress and anxiety are not feelings to be fought, and may be red flags that something is drastically awry in one's situation. They may be indicators that we need to take a mental inventory, looking critically at our lifestyle, and ask ourselves some difficult questions. They can call us to turn our attention inward.

Today's society has become comfortable with our increased experience of both stress and anxiety, often considering it to be a normal by-product of a successful or productive lifestyle. Certain stress-producing situations may be out of our control, though the number of situations for which that is actually true is fewer than we tend to perceive (see Learned Helplessness p. 75). Our health and well-being are regularly placed as our lowest priority in relation to our goals, and we often engage in conflict, or unhealthily internalize issues that would better remain external. Ironically, the times when we are involved in stressful situations seem to be the times when we are less likely to seek out our enjoyments or relaxation activities—the exact opposite behavioral reaction to what is truly needed.

While the experiences of anxiety and stress are natural and inherently useful, they are obviously quite unhealthy when allowed to continue for extended periods of time. People who dwell on worst-case scenarios, who exaggerate perceived risks, or who project doubt and undue worry are artificially employing anxiety, thus continually keeping their fight or flight response in an activated mode. This has the effect of calling to the brain for help, keeping it in a state of continual arousal when no help is truly needed. What ensues is sickness.

Panics and Phobias

In February 2003, what began as a night of music and fireworks in a club in Rhode Island, quickly turned dark. The fireworks went awry, and within three minutes the show turned into a blaze.

There were no sprinklers in the venue, which soon filled with black smoke. Panic quickly set in. The crowd rushed to the front entrance. There were stories of people risking their lives to save others. However, there were also signs of trampling, especially at the door. Of the 96 who died that night, most died at the front door, where people had blindly followed one another in sheer terror to the place where they had entered. Sadly, the club had four other functioning entrances.

Understanding Panic

Panic is an emotional state of blinding fear. It is one that overcomes an individual, replacing all rational and logical thought and often leading people to take actions that they would never otherwise contemplate, even actions that are harmful to their own well-being.

What Causes Panic?

Stressful life events can be catalysts that trigger panic disorders,

where an individual may suffer one or even repeated panic attacks. In the course of a panic attack the "fight or flight" reaction is triggered, but often with no direct stimulus. In an attack, an individual experiences complete and all-consuming anxiety, the physical symptoms of which closely resemble a heart attack. Such symptoms may include a rapid heart rate, chest pains, trembling, dizziness, shortness of breath, and nausea. A panic episode often begins abruptly, without warning, and peaks in about 10 minutes.

Panic Attacks

There are three types of panic attacks: spontaneous, specific, and situational. In the case of spontaneous attacks, there is no direct stimulus. General stress or specific loss is thought to lessen a person's overall threshold, and in this state their underlying physiology becomes predisposed for the switch to flip, and an attack to be triggered.

•••• Being trapped in an elevator could trigger a **panic attack**.

In specific and situational attacks, there is a given stimulus that triggers the attack. An attack brought on by exposure to a personal phobia is an example of a specific panic attack, which is likely to develop in places or situations where previous panic attacks have occurred. A situational attack will also occur under particular circumstances; but, whereas a particular catalyst may trigger a situational attack, it is not the object of the panic itself.

As with anxiety, healthy fear is a natural emotion likely designed to protect and direct the self in threatening situations. Babies appear to be naturally afraid of certain potentially threatening stimuli, such as snakes and heights, for example, while they learn over time to be afraid of man-made objects such as guns. It is likely that the development of phobias is a natural response to fear that has gone awry.

A similar model to the disturbances found in panic attacks may be the cause of phobias—extreme fear in specific situations in which there is no real danger, or where the sense of fear is significantly out of proportion to the risk.

There are two theories on the nature of phobias: The non-associative model holds that vulnerability to phobias is largely innate, and does not arise directly from environmental experience. However, some theories hold that phobias are a result of transmission from others, or social conditioning. Interestingly, some studies have found that certain phobias may be hereditary.

Overcoming Anxiety

Techniques for overcoming phobias and panic attacks may employ education, psychotherapy, and medication. Exposure to the particular stimulus is generally an important part of treatment. Two examples are "systematic desensitization," a treatment in which the subject is gradually exposed to the fear, albeit largely in imagined and simulated situations; and "flooding," where the subject is exposed to the feared stimuli.

Post-Traumatic Stress Disorder

Imagine your worst nightmare. Imagine it coming true. Now imagine not being able to stop imagining it. This is what happens to victims of post-traumatic stress disorder (see pp. 38–39). Symptoms of this debilitating disorder include hallucinations, flashbacks, and vividly accurate dreams.

A Brief History of Trauma

Initially known as "shell shock," the modern-day condition known as post-traumatic stress disorder (PTSD) was first diagnosed among survivors of combat. PTSD is a condition that can result when an individual is involved with a potentially life-threatening event or events, or where grave bodily or emotional harm was potentially suffered by oneself or others. Examples of such traumatic experiences include exposure to severe violence, crime, or warfare, natural disasters, serious accidents, and witnessing trauma to others.

What is PTSD?

The condition of PTSD fundamentally may be disorder of affect-arousal regulation. In other words, once the arousal system becomes flooded, as is the case in a traumatic situation, a switch becomes stuck and can no longer return to "normal," even after the stimulus is removed. This switch, and the patient, remain in constant reactive mode. It is possible that PTSD victims re-experience their traumas repeatedly as the stimuli they experienced overloaded the

•••• A soldier suffering from **PTSD** may need specialist counseling to help process and come to terms with the experiences of war.

abilities of their cognitive processes, and the brain was unable to consolidate or regulate the related memories and emotions. It is thought that this continual re-experience may be the result of attempts by an oversaturated system to process the still-undigested information.

The shockingly accurate dreams, in which a trauma is played out exactly as it happened, seem to further support the idea of undigested or unprocessed information. The normal encoding that is evident in dream states, the non-linear and non-precise dream storylines that we are all accustomed to—where memories are processed and consolidated—is strikingly absent in the dreams of trauma sufferers.

Why Does This Happen to Some Victims, but Not to All?
......

Two people may experience the same trauma, but be affected by it in drastically different ways. One may simply be "shaken up" but not develop the full-blown symptoms of PTSD, while the other is traumatized and suffers the condition at its worst. Why is this? Research shows associations between PTSD and poorer neurocognitive function, especially involving attention and memory. These deficits are thought to be the consequence of abnormalities in the norepinephrine (a hormone and neurotransmitter) system or of decreased volume in the hippocampus region of the brain, which is associated with PTSD. The

question is, do these abnormalities cause a greater vulnerability and likelihood of PTSD occurring in the case of trauma, or does the trauma itself cause these abnormalities? Are individuals with greater memory abilities more successful at suppressing the unwanted intrusive thoughts of PTSD? This has been a very difficult question to answer, as by its very nature trauma itself is unpredictable.

An Eternal Struggle
....

Other complications keep PTSD sufferers trapped in their continual struggles as well. Everyday experiences may be perceived as part of the triggering trauma, and an intense, irrational tendency to avoid anything that is remotely related to the trauma may ensue. For example, a backfiring car may be experienced as a gun being fired, or a woman who has been attacked when returning to her car after shopping may be unable to go anywhere alone.

Sufferers may have an exaggerated "startle" response. They are likely to experience disconnectedness especially from their sense of self, and struggle to find the feelings, interest, or inclination to care much about anything. They may suddenly find it hard to imagine any sense of their future. They may withdraw, and practice avoidance of anything that might trigger their response. Traumatized individuals are constantly oscillating between re-experiencing the trauma and trying to avoid it.

Herbert Benson

For much of medical history, alternative concepts have been scoffed at by traditional, conservative medicine. Practices such as acupuncture, meditation, or yoga were thought of as "far out," the realm of hippies or weirdos. Today, many of these practices are well respected.

agreed to explore the effects of meditation in a laboratory setting. He showed that it was indeed possible to lower patients' blood pressure voluntarily. The process they found that achieved this result, was termed the "relaxation response."

The simple fact that the meditative process was shown to evoke the healing process opened the doors for greater awareness of how our thoughts can impact on our physical well-being.

Herbert Benson is an American cardiologist who is largely credited with giving credence to the healing power that the mind can have over the body. While researching cardiology at Harvard, Dr. Benson was approached by Transcendental Meditators. They believed that they could control their blood pressure through their meditative thoughts. At the time, the cardiovascular system was thought to be completely autonomic (functioning automatically on its own). However, Dr. Benson

Dr. Benson speaks of the mind being able to "disconnect" from everyday thoughts and worries, calming people's bodies and minds more quickly and to a degree otherwise unachievable. Once the mind reaches a state of deep relaxation, the body is able to relax and repair some of its most important mechanisms, and increase overall immunity.

Regular **meditation** calms the body, and can even lower blood pressure.

He also stresses the importance of the "faith factor," and has claimed that a spiritual belief system increases the benefits and transports the mind–body even more dramatically, quieting worries and fears significantly better than the relaxation response alone. He pushes no one belief system over another, but preaches the importance of tuning in to your feelings and trusting your instincts more often. Benson encourages people to commit to their own processes of finding out what is important to them, whether through "listening to one's heart," "praying," or "sleeping on it." Some people act on instincts or common sense; others find a truth or intuition emerges slowly. But most people know when something "feels right."

According to Benson, trusting the power of this process is paramount in "letting go" of worries and stressors, and embracing thorough relaxation. Such relaxation processes are also quite useful in treating stress and anxiety disorders.

ACHIEVING THE RELAXATION RESPONSE

Try these steps adapted from the Benson-Henry Institute for Mind Body Medicine:

1. Sit quietly in a comfortable position.

2. Close your eyes.

3. Relax all your muscles, beginning with your feet and progressing up to your face.

4. Breathe through your nose. Become aware of your breathing. As you breathe out, say the word "om"—or any soothing sound, preferably with no particular meaning or association—silently to yourself. For example, breathe in… out, "om"; in… out, "om"; and so on. Breathe easily and naturally.

5. Continue for 10-20 minutes. You may open your eyes to check the time, but do not use an alarm. When you finish, sit quietly for a few minutes, first with your eyes closed and later with your eyes opened. Do not stand for a few minutes.

6. Do not worry about whether you achieve a deep level of relaxation. Maintain a passive attitude and permit relaxation to occur at its own pace. When distracting thoughts occur, try to ignore them and return to repeating "om."

With practice, the response should come with little effort. Practice the technique once or twice a day, but not within two hours after a meal, since the digestive processes seem to interfere.

Chilling For All the Right Reasons

The effects of emotional unease on our physical health are widespread and clear as day. Continuous emotional unrest, regardless of how much we may focus on it, affects our mental, physical, and spiritual health negatively. Stress and anxiety can increase blood pressure, interfere with digestive processes, cause muscular tension and resulting complications, and contribute to heart disease and other medical problems.

Anxiety can be the beginning of a dangerous downward spiral if ignored, and often the symptoms are suppressed or accepted as a normal part of one's reality. Symptoms of stress or anxiety such as irritability, disrupted sleep, muscle tension, restlessness, inability to concentrate, nausea, regular head- or stomachaches, and ulcers, are often not taken seriously. The reality is that they are often red flags through which our body communicates to us that something in our lives, or our internal processing of our external environment, is not right and needs changing.

Stress can interrupt sleep, and quickly spiral into a vicious cycle of trying to catch up on lost sleep during the day then lying wide awake at night.

LEARNING TO RELAX

If these symptoms of stress and anxiety occur frequently and interfere with your physical and emotional well-being, then it may be time to learn a healthier way to cope with anxiety. Relaxation techniques can especially help patients with cardiac disease, hypertension, anger, angina, arrhythmia, diabetes, pain, high cholesterol, sleep problems, stress-related disorders, and even those who are preparing for or recovering from surgery. Relaxation is shown to promote long-term health and improve the quality of life in patients dealing with serious health problems.

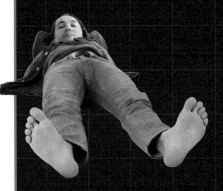

Therapeutic relaxation techniques help teach the mind to slow down and focus on breathing in order to reconnect with the body. The purpose is to bring our bodies back to a state of equilibrium, or balance, following disruptions that put stress on all the systems the body regulates. This is done by learning to reach a state of "thoughtless awareness" from intrusive thoughts and maintaining focus on the body sensations that produce muscular and mental release.

There are many types of relaxation techniques and it is important to find the one(s) that work best for you. Here are just a few examples:

Progressive Muscle Relaxation
Visualization
Deep Abdominal Breathing
Guided Imagery
Art Therapy
Meditation
Yoga
Aromatherapy
Music Therapy
Prayer

There are also a number of tests to take online to see how many symptoms of stress and anxiety apply to you. Typing "anxiety risk assessment" into a search engine will provide you with plenty of examples.

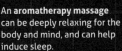

An **aromatherapy massage** can be deeply relaxing for the body and mind, and can help induce sleep.

8

Sleep

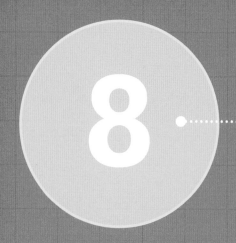

Add up all the time you spend snoozing in bed and it comes to years and years. You'd think we'd all be experts, and yet many people's lives are blighted by sleep problems including insomnia, sleepwalking, and nightmares. This chapter explores what happens if we don't get the sleep we need, as well providing tips for how to get a good night's slumber.

Sleep Parasomnias

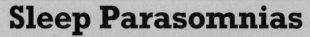

Stan Taylor was principal of one of the largest high schools in a medium-sized city. He was well known and well liked, always knowing students' names and having a smile or a kind word for those he passed. He was a respected figure in the local community. He was happily married for 30 years, having raised three successful children. Faces drained white the morning Mrs. Taylor walked into her office with bruises and scratches all up and down her arms and face. "What on earth happened?" her colleagues cried out. "Who did this to you?" Mrs. Taylor looked down, not knowing how to respond. Slowly, she looked up, tears filling her eyes. "Stan did," she whispered. Gasps of disbelief filled the room. "He…" she stammered, "he was… asleep."

Stan Taylor is an example of the most commonly studied parasomnia, REM Sleep Behavior Disorder (RBD) where the person is in rapid eye movement (REM) sleep and acts out violent dreams through body movements and sounds.

What's Happening?

In essence, this is a state of partial arousal. The body displays behaviors associated with being awake and asleep, simultaneously. During these phenomena called parasomnias, a person will perform what are often complex physical and verbal behaviors, including ones that are dangerous—all while in the mind–body state that we define as sleep.

BEHAVIORS ACTED OUT IN RBD CAN INCLUDE:

Yelling
Cursing
Punching
Strangling
Driving
Firing guns
and more...

There tends to be a correlation between the acted-out behavior and subject content reported in a dream.

The Case of Mr. Dorff

One of the strangest and most famous examples of sleep parasomnia is the case of Mr. Dorff. He was a retired grocer who sought treatment at the Mayo Clinic in Minnesota for what he called his "violent moving nightmares." Indeed his nightmares were literally both violent and moving, and in one dream Mr. Dorff ran smack into his bedroom dresser believing that he was a quarterback on the verge of making a touchdown.

Causes of Parasomnias

Why are these physiological systems aroused at inappropriate times? In 1953, Nathaniel Kleitman and his assistant Eugene Aserinsky found that measurements from an electroencephalogram (a device for measuring electrical activity in the brain), during the REM stage of sleep in which the majority of dreaming occurs, gave readings similar to the pattern of electrical activity that is seen during wakefulness.

Although not all parasomnia behavior takes place in REM sleep, scientists have found that during REM the brain sends the same signals to muscles to perform the movements that would be accurate if the person were awake. For most people, during REM sleep another brain circuit simultaneously sends inhibitory chemical signals to the muscles, paralyzing them so as not to perform the instructions. This inhibition applies to all muscles in the body except the diaphragm, one small muscle in the ear, and the muscles that move the eyes. Neurons in certain areas of the mid-brain are known to suppress movement and are implicated in some parasomnias. Interestingly, it is the same region affected in sufferers of Parkinson's disease, and a disproportionate number of parasomnia sufferers develop Parkinson's disease later in life, further supporting the theory that this area of the brain is responsible.

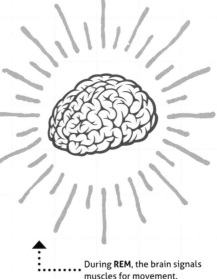

During **REM**, the brain signals muscles for movement.

Behind the physical causes lie deeper reasons such as biological dysfunction, stress, and depression—which between them are some of the most common underlying factors. It is also interesting to note that parasomnias tend to be more common in children than adults, and can sometimes run in families.

Sleep Deprivation

We can easily notice the effect of even minimal sleep deprivation. Our thoughts don't seem as sharp, our motor responses seem slow, and our moods are easily affected. In fact there is an undeniable connection between our sleep and our mood, and the link between clinical depression and disrupted sleep is nearly perfect—it is worth noting that disruption of normal sleep is one of the primary criteria for a diagnosis of depression.

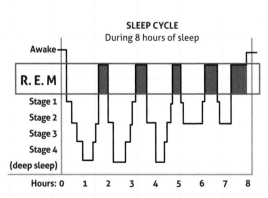

It is also worth considering the impact of extreme deprivation on torture victims who are forced to remain awake for extended periods of time, and who report visual and auditory hallucinations as they near the brink of madness. The complications of insomnia and sleep deprivation are multifold, and it is obvious to us all that without proper sleep it's nearly impossible to have a proper mood. But why? Why should fatigue not be able to exist independently from mood disturbance?

The Pattern of Sleep

With both insomnia and excessive sleep, as occurs in depression, it's not simply a matter of more or less time spent in sleep. The whole normal, healthy sleep cycle is torn to pieces.

The pattern of healthy sleep includes four to six separate cycles per night through periods of progressively deeper, more relaxing, slow-wave sleep, which are interspersed with stages of REM sleep that involve high amounts of brain activity and rapid eye movements.

SLEEP CYCLE
During 8 hours of sleep

Awake	
R.E.M	
Stage 1	
Stage 2	
Stage 3	
Stage 4	
(deep sleep)	
Hours: 0 1 2 3 4 5 6 7 8	

The Purpose of Sleep

One of the functions of sleep is to facilitate the consolidation of memory. REM sleep has been found to be involved with emotional memory. Sleep researchers have found that depressed people enter the REM stage more quickly than normal. They then stay in it longer, and experience more brain activity than normal. Researchers believe that in clinical depression, the loss of slow-wave sleep and the rush to REM sleep have a detrimental effect on the way memories consolidate and the way that the REM system regulates mood. The increase in REM sleep in the depressed is thought to lead to an over-consolidation of negative memory, causing the sleeper to wake with an extra amount of bad things to think about, because the negative feelings have not been processed and stored away properly.

The disturbances are thought to interfere with the perception of reality around the time of falling sleep, causing patients with insomnia to overestimate the time it takes them to fall asleep and underestimate the amount of time they actually spend sleeping.

Insomnia is the most common sleep disorder, and people who suffer from it have difficulty both falling and staying asleep. It is worth noting that those who suffer from insomnia usually average six full hours of sleep—not a desperately small amount, yet little enough to disrupt the normal sleep cycle, which is where the problems start to arise.

Driving while **sleep deprived** is hazardous as you risk nodding off at the wheel.

Sleep disturbance results in reduced concentration and decreased reaction time during waking hours, leading to reduced productivity and greater risk of accidents. Amazingly, insomnia affects around a third of adults at some point in their lives, especially during periods of stress. Chronic insomnia is thankfully less common; it may be caused by a number of factors in addition to stress, including imbalances in body chemistry or other medical conditions.

Sleepwalking and Sleeptalking

Although frequently a source of amusement, the twin problems of sleepwalking and sleeptalking can have serious consequences, and also provide interesting insights into the sleeping brain.

Try reading any text while singing your favorite song and you will find it is nearly impossible to gain the full meaning of the sentences while simultaneously recalling and singing the song. That is because your focus is divided, meaning you cannot fully tune in to the two channels at once. This is the same in normal sleep, where sleeping inhibits other active processes. However, in parasomnias such as sleepwalking and talking in one's sleep it appears as if the opposite is taking place—in these malfunctions it is almost as if the brain is attempting to tune in to two very separate frequencies at the same time.

Sleepwalking

The medical term for sleepwalking is somnambulism, a parasomnia that most often occurs during deep, non-REM sleep early in the night. If it occurs during REM sleep, it is part of REM behavior disorder and tends to happen closer to morning.

The process of sleepwalking involves a sudden arousal from non-REM sleep. When someone sleepwalks, they may sit up and look as though they are awake. They may get up, walk around, or even perform complex activities such as moving furniture, brushing teeth, or even driving. A sleepwalking episode can last from just a few seconds or minutes to over a half-hour.

Myth has it that it can be dangerous to awaken a sleepwalker: This is not true, though the person may be confused or disoriented upon awakening. Another misconception is that sleepwalkers cannot be injured; in reality sleepwalkers often hurt themselves through falling and tripping.

A **sleepwalker** may perform everyday tasks such as cleaning or getting dressed.

Symptoms of Sleepwalking

The first clue that someone may be sleepwalking is that they have their eyes open when they otherwise appear asleep—they may have a blank look on their face, or may sit up and appear awake. They may walk around and engage in detailed activity. However, sleepwalkers do not remember the episode upon awakening, and will be disoriented if awakened suddenly.

Sleepwalking can occur at any age, but occurs most often in children aged between four and eight, and appears to run in families.

Sleeptalking

Medically known as somniloquy, this sleep disorder does not appear to be detrimental to the sleeptalker's mental or physical well-being. Although classified as a parasomnia, talking during sleep is generally considered of no medical or psychological consequence, and people who talk while asleep have no awareness that they are talking. Often they will wake when their sleeptalking startles another person, who then makes a noise at being woken up, waking the sleeptalker to ask the other "What's wrong?"

Sleeptalking can occur at any point in the sleep cycle, though the lighter the sleep stage, the more intelligible the speech tends to be. In light sleep people may have entire conversations; however, in heavy sleep they may be restricted to moans and gibberish. It is still unknown whether the talking is closely linked to dreaming, though people intuitively associate sleeptalking with dreaming. While it is possible to talk in REM sleep, it isn't as likely as at other stages due to the muscular inhibition during the REM cycle, which usually immobilizes the jaw and speech mechanisms.

Sleeptalking that is related to RBD or sleep terrors is much more dramatic than that seen otherwise. As a part of RBD, talking may be loud and emotional. Talking during sleep terrors tends to involve intense fear, with sufferers screaming and shouting.

What's the Problem?

Somniloquy is not generally considered a serious problem unless other disorders, such as somnambulism and apnea, are involved. However, anxiety disorders, stress, and fevers often make people talk more. The cause of somniloquy is unknown, but around 5 percent of adults are reported to talk regularly in their sleep. If you're one of those, then the following may help to decrease sleeptalking: avoiding heavy meals before bedtime; reducing stress levels; and practicing healthy sleep patterns.

Life Without Dreams

Our dreams, our deepest desires for ourselves, our ideal future—what would life be like without dreams?

In the Absence of Dreams

Though it is known that most people do dream every night—given normal functioning brain status—there is a wide variation in people's ability to recall their dreams, which is the reason behind some people believing that they do not dream. Studies on patients who literally do not dream due to brain damage in specific locales, however, have provided interesting information about the nature of dreams themselves.

Damage to an area in the forebrain responsible for spatial recognition and the generation of imagery (the inferior parietal lobe) can be responsible for the brain not entering a dream sequence—hardly a surprising finding given the image-based nature of dreams. However, it is also interesting to note that when damage occurs to an area in the white matter at the bottom of the frontal lobes that drives motivation, dreams are also stopped.

Remembering Your Dreams

It is when we awaken during highly active REM sleep that we have the sudden feeling of "switching gears,"

where we wake up in what seems to be the middle of a dream, or wake up saying "I was just having a dream about…" For a period of time, one's memory accessing the dream is at its clearest, and details can be recounted at a level that soon fades away.

There is a wide variation among people's abilities to recall dream content, and it is indeed an imperfect science, but for those who have poor dream recall, exercises can be employed to help. (See panel opposite.) It is thought that fear of nightmares, or other anxieties or misguided beliefs about dreams and the unconscious, can block dream recall, and these can usually be overcome by learning about the useful nature of dreams and by recognizing that the majority of nightmares may represent opportunities for personal healing through much-needed emotional release.

Jot down details of your dream as soon as you awaken.

IMPROVING YOUR DREAM RECALL

Here are a few tips to help you improve your dream recall:

Keep a dream journal next to your bed. The moment you awaken, or at any time that you are struck with memories of a dream, record as much detail as you can recall. Include images, feelings, words utilized. This technique is shown to improve over time. Include notes about your own recent emotional state, things or people that have been on your mind, and the quality of your sleep. Look for patterns or recurring themes in your dreams.

Stay in bed for 15 minutes after waking—this may help you remember dream details.

Use meditation and relaxation exercises to help tap into your subconscious mind.

Assert that you will remember your dreams when you are still awake.

Visualize your dreams.

Setting an alarm to wake you periodically during the night may keep your brainwave activity at a higher rate. Periodic waking may allow you to catch yourself in the act of dreaming and record it quickly. However, while this may help improve your dream recall it is not particularly advisable, as it will impair the quality of your sleep, perhaps resulting in some of the symptoms of sleep deprivation discussed on pages 130–131.

The most important element of trying to remember your dreams is actively cultivating awareness through consistent practice of the above exercises.

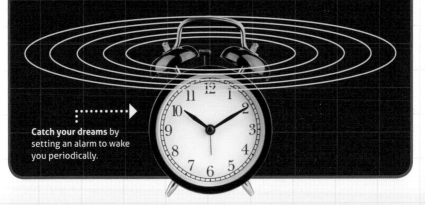

Catch your dreams by setting an alarm to wake you periodically.

Nightmares

••••••••••••••••••••••••••••••••••

Dreams, and especially "bad" dreams, can help make us aware of the things that we may be most psychologically entrenched in. The dreams themselves may serve to process some of the issues, and can serve as a guide to what we should focus on to remedy our current struggles.

DO YOU RECOGNIZE ANY OF THESE DREAMS?

It is difficult to know just how dreams link to our waking lives, but that hasn't stopped psychologists from trying to find out— one of the most famous books in the field is Freud's *The Interpretation of Dreams*.

Here are some common dream themes and their interpretations. Try to re-experience the feeling of your dream, and be aware of similar feelings in your waking life.

Dream One: You tend to have dreams where you are being chased or under attack.
Interpretation: Being chased or under attack may indicate part of your personality you have not paid attention to, the existence of repressed feelings, or part of the past that you feel is unresolved.

Dream Two: You are on stage and don't know your lines, or you are unprepared for a final exam.
Interpretation: Examine aspects of your life or yourself where you are not feeling confident or where you feel embarrassed.

Dream Three: You are invisible or need help and cannot get anyone's attention.

Interpretation: Do you feel like you are not making an impact in your world, or are you feeling disrespected?

Dream Four: You are falling.
Interpretation Are you weighted down by responsibilities? Are you feeling unsupported, or ungrounded?

Dream Five:
There is an accident or disaster.
Interpretation: Does something feel outside of your abilities of control? Are you overextended?

Dream Six: You dream of injury to your body.
Interpretation: Are you feeling guilty or neglectful in some area of your life (other than the body)?

Dream Seven You are searching for someone or something you cannot find.
Interpretation: Are you feeling dissatisfied?

CONTROL YOUR DREAMS, CONTROL YOUR LIFE

Some think that listening to what your dreaming self is saying can allow a subtle but powerful control over your waking life. It can also improve the quality of your dreams. Using the techniques described on page 135, try bringing more awareness to your dreaming life with the following steps:

1. Deliberately cultivate a relationship with your dreaming self.

2. Just prior to sleeping, dedicate a given amount of time to the process.

3. Create a peaceful space; use dim lighting or candles.

4. Select an issue that's been on your mind. Focus on the issue, rehearsing and repeating the thoughts in your mind.

5. Create images in your mind of things associated with the issue. Gather photos, newspaper clippings, anything concrete that represents the issue. Stare at the objects or close your eyes and focus in your mind's eye.

6. Visualize yourself taking control of the situation. Guide both your real-life experience and the dream process. If you dreamed you were trapped in a sinking box last night, envision yourself bursting out of the box and swimming toward the finish line of a triathlon. Visualize your outcomes, seeing yourself in what you envision things to be like when they have been changed.

7. Try deep-breathing exercises or the steps used to elicit the relaxation response (see p. 123) to amplify your results.

8. Imagine your dreaming self taking control in your dreams; keep a journal of your desired results.

9. Dedicate yourself to this process.

10. Sweet dreams!

Visualizing a **positive outcome** to your dreams, such as escaping from a sinking box, can help empower your waking life.

Stanley Coren

Stanley Coren is a psychologist who has done extensive research on sleep habits and the often disastrous results of our sleep-deprived society. He challenges the notion that sleep deprivation is a mere inconvenience—as it is generally dismissed in today's world—and portrays the cumulative sleep debt we develop with continued lack of sleep as a much larger and pervasive detrimental influence on human efficiency and function.

Coren asserts that individuals require 8–10 hours of sleep per 24-hour period, which is what occurs in natural circumstances free from the interference of artificial light sources. The average sleep period seen throughout most modern industrial societies is 7–7.5 hours. Coren also believes we operate from a framework of cumulative sleep debt which gets worse and worse as time continues if our full sleep needs are not met.

Daylight-saving time creates an unnatural and significant jump in our sleep cycle, according to Coren. One of his studies shows that the numbers of traffic accidents increase by about 7 percent during the days following the hour change and industrial accidents increase by around 6 percent.

Sleeping Baby

Coren notes that a newborn baby will sleep for 16–20 hours per day in what is a very active and animated

sleep. Newborns are thought to spend 50 percent of their sleeping time dreaming, a fact that completely puzzled scientists. If dreamwork is meant for the purpose of consolidating memory and working out situations encountered during the day, how could a newborn who is awake so few hours and has so little to process need so much "processing" time? Coren cites results of studies that show that babies in utero at 25 weeks dream nearly all the time. It is held that reams serve to stimulate parts of the brain in the unstimulating environment of the womb, and are thought to assist in the development of brain tissue. Dreams "exercise" the infant's senses, so upon entering the world the adjustment is much less shocking!

Newborns may dream for 50 percent of the time they sleep each day.

DISTURBING TALES FROM THE FILES OF SLEEP DEPRIVATION

In his 1997 book *Sleep Thieves*, Stanley Coren details a number of different case studies in which the effects of sleep deprivation are startlingly profound. Here are just two examples:

Sleepless in Surgery

Until recently, medical residents regularly worked 100-hour weeks, frequently entailing continuous shifts of 24-36 hours. In Denver in 1995, anesthesiologist Joseph Verbrugge Jr. was charged with manslaughter and held responsible for the death of an eight-year-old boy undergoing a routine ear operation. Witness testimony held that Dr. Verbrugge fell asleep several times during the surgery, remaining asleep in one instance for 20 minutes. Since he was asleep, he did not notice the alarming change in vital signs until he awoke, too late.

Keep on Trucking

A truck driver named Joe recounted that his work involved two to three weeks on the road per trip, where distances of 900 miles per day were needed. Some jobs held bonuses for early arrival, or penalties for late delivery. Joe tells his worst story, driving across the flatland of Utah, where he started to feel some bumps in the road and couldn't find the white line. He eventually stopped and fell asleep. He awoke to flashing lights and an officer pounding on the door. Joe's truck had been spotted by a patrol plane. It was ten miles off the highway, in the middle of nowhere. Joe guessed he must have fallen asleep and driven off course.

Edison's Curse

Society's drastic reduction in sleep habits largely resulted from the invention of the lightbulb. In fact, Edison actively touted the fact that he never slept more than four to five hours a day, and strongly asserted his view that people who slept more hours were lazy.

Healthy Sleep

If you are hitting the snooze button in the morning, it means you are not getting enough sleep. Don't laugh. If you are getting enough sleep, you wake up easily and automatically, refreshed. For our sleep-deprived societies it may seem like a fantasy world, but this should be the norm.

HOW TO GET A GOOD NIGHT'S SLEEP

Set a regular schedule: Since our sleep-wake cycle is regulated by our circadian (daily) "clock" in our brain, many people with regular sleep schedules find they often wake up a minute or two before the alarm is set to sound. Keeping the same schedule, ideally including weekends, strengthens the circadian function, helps with sleep onset at night, and improves regularity of sleep cycles, which helps with overall sleep quality.

Set the scene: A relaxing routine before bedtime can help prepare your senses and your body for sleep. Relaxation activities can include those already discussed, along with herbal tea or warm milk, yoga, meditation, soaking in a hot bath. Pursue your pre-bedtime routine in dim lighting, and avoid bright lighting which signals to the brain that it should be getting alert as it would in the morning, not winding down.

No more pillow talk: Avoid stimulating activities before bedtime, including exciting television shows, intense reading, bill paying, or having emotionally invigorating conversations.

Control yourself: Distractions such as street noise, street lights, or a partner snoring can make it difficult to enter or remain in deep sleep. While it may initially be difficult to get used to earplugs, eye shades, or noise machines (that drown out other noise), taking measures to control external activation can be beneficial in getting a good night's rest.

Avoid looking at the clock: This tends to cause anxiety through worrying that you won't get a good night's sleep. The anxiety itself then makes it difficult to fall asleep.

Use the bed only for sleeping.

Exercise, but not within three hours of bedtime.

Avoid caffeine or stimulants before sleep. They can affect the sleep pattern even when it's not perceptible to you when awake. Likewise, alcohol should be avoided before bedtime; even though it is thought of as a sedative, it keeps you in the light stages of sleep. Also avoid heavy eating or rich foods before bedtime.

A Short History of Sleep

For much of our history, sleep was considered a single block of time when our brain and body turned off, giving us a rest. However, over the past few decades, we have gained the understanding that the brain is very much active while the "body" sleeps, and know that there are very distinct things that happen in different stages of sleep. We know that certain stages help us feel energized and focused the next day, while other stages consolidate memory, or affect mood regulation. Furthermore, deep sleep triggers release of growth hormone, which fuels growth in children, and helps build muscle mass and repair cells and tissues in children and adults.

Another type of hormone, levels of which are increased during sleep, works to fight various infections, which may explain why, when your body is sick, all it wants to do is sleep, and why healthy sleep habits help keep you from getting sick. The hormones released during sleep also affect how the body uses energy, and studies find that the less people sleep, the more likely they are to be overweight or obese, to develop diabetes, and to prefer eating foods that are high in calories and carbohydrates.

So, now you know, deciding to take that extra hour to work, clean, party, or stay up to study for an exam, may just end up costing you more than you think.

A good night's sleep is important for **re-energizing** the body.

Index
· · · · · · · · ·

Credits
· · · · · · · · · · ·